'Nicky is a hero to so many Indigenous footballers. His story is one that cannot be missed.' **Tony Armstrong**

'Raw, authentic, honest and utterly unputdownable!' **Paul Kelly, singer/songwriter**

'A compelling account from the fleet-footed footballer who ran like the wind down the wing and stood strong against the rip tide of racism a generation before Adam Goodes. Winmar's is at once a heroic and sad tale that all football fans, nay all Australians, must read if they are to understand their game and their country. A great read.' **Peter Lalor**

'Honest, moving, painful, funny: Nicky Winmar's book holds nothing back. Matthew Hardy has got right under the most famous skin in football.' **Gideon Haigh**

'I loved watching Nicky Winmar play, and I'll never forget the unsettling mixture of shame and pride I felt when he faced down the racist crowd with his unforgettable gesture of defiance. Reading Nicky's story, with its insights into the pain and rage behind his iconic moment, the shame persists but my admiration has only grown. Once we watched him in wonder. And now it's time to listen and learn.' **Tim Winton**

**Neil Elvis 'Nicky' Winmar** is a former Australian rules footballer best known for his career at St Kilda and the Western Bulldogs in the Australian Football League, as well as South Fremantle in the West Australian Football League. In twelve seasons with St Kilda, Winmar won the club's best and fairest award in 1989 and 1995 and was named in the Team of the Year/All-Australian team three times. Having represented Western Australia in eight interstate matches, Winmar was named in St Kilda's Team of the Century in 2003 and was inducted into the AFL Hall of Fame in 2022.

**Matthew Hardy** is the author of the bestselling childhood memoir *Saturday Afternoon Fever*, still on sale after 25 years. Matthew has had his writing published in *Esquire* and *The Independent* in the UK, as well as *The Age*, *The Guardian* and the *Herald Sun* in Australia. During a decade in London, Matthew wrote for projects with and for Ricky Gervais and Kelsey Grammar, and was part of the team who won ITV's first ever BAFTA Award. Matthew loves being the father of his two delightful daughters, Ruby and Cleopatra, and brother to Mark and Simon.

# NICKY WINMAR

WITH **MATTHEW HARDY**

# MY STORY

FROM BUSH KID TO AFL LEGEND

ALLEN&UNWIN

SYDNEY·MELBOURNE·AUCKLAND·LONDON

Allen & Unwin
Cammeraygal Country
83 Alexander Street
Crows Nest NSW 2065
Australia
Phone: (61 2) 8425 0100
Email:   info@allenandunwin.com
Web:     www.allenandunwin.com

*Allen & Unwin acknowledges the Traditional Owners of the Country on which we live and work. We pay our respects to all Aboriginal and Torres Strait Islander Elders, past and present.*

A catalogue record for this book is available from the National Library of Australia

ISBN 978 1 76106 516 3

Index by Puddingburn Publishing Services
Set in 12.75/18.5 pt Adobe Garamond by Midland Typesetters, Australia
Printed and bound in Australia by the Opus Group

10 9 8 7 6 5 4 3 2 1

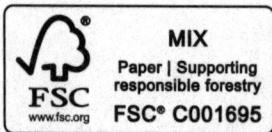

*I'd like to say thank you to my ex-wife Kelly, the mother of our kind and clever children, Tynan and Shakira. I know I wasn't easy to live with.*

*I've often barely understood myself so how was anyone else supposed to understand me?*

*I had baggage back then and there's still more to unpack yet.*

*Thank you, Kelly, for putting up with me as long as you did and for bringing up our wonderful kids.*

*Thank you and all my love to Tynan and Shakira.*

*Thanks also to my lovely daughter Benita.*

*To everyone I've just mentioned, as Elvis once sang, you were always on my mind.*

# CONTENTS

# PROLOGUE

I may have been a Saint but I've fought a lot of demons. This one right now is the most evil of them all. He exists as the gun in my hand, the pain in my head and the hurt in my heart. I'm going to end it all. My wife is trying to get into the house but I've locked the place up tight. We've had an argument but that's not the reason. I've been waiting for an excuse and this latest scenario seems as good as any. My wife has nothing to do with this mood. These demons surrounded me before we even met each other. I'm married, we have a house and I'm a professional footballer, so I should be happy, right? Or at the very least I shouldn't be so sad. My constant urge to self-sabotage has overpowered me . . .

I've recently read the formerly big-drinking Jimmy Barnes's brilliant bestselling first book, and it's apparent that like him I had a dad who was a big drinker. It didn't do Barnsey's dad any good and it didn't do Barnsey any good. It didn't do me or my dad any good either. Didn't stop us though. Did any of us have understandable reasons? Probably none you'd want to hear, or if you did hear them you'd wish you hadn't. Were we unable or unwilling to quit? Who knows, but for those people who are hurting, alcohol can feel like it soothes the soul, and the best part is that it can create that feeling quickly. The problem is that too much alcohol leads to more pain than it numbs. For you and for those you love.

. . . So, I'm trying to pluck up the courage—or is it the cowardice?—to finish myself off. It's a dark hole that needs to be filled with light rather than liquor. But it's like they say, sometimes the light at the end of the tunnel can seem like a train coming the other way. The panicked sound of my wife's shouting and the banging on the door has now dissolved. I can't hear a sound. I can't think a thought. I can't feel a thing aside from my finger on the trigger of this gun.

# INTRODUCTION

Before I began writing this book, I wanted to determine exactly why I should do it, and why anybody would want to read it.

The answer came in two forms.

Maybe people who are interested in how an athlete reaches the top of their chosen sport and then stays there—and how people set about achieving their lifelong goals, be they sporting or otherwise—might also gain some insight on Indigenous Australians.

Maybe people might simply seek insight on Indigenous Australians, sporting or otherwise.

I also wanted to try to gain some insight into myself, and ideally, learn from my failures while also celebrating my successes.

The *Washington Post* recently reported that California's esteemed Chapman University surveyed thousands of people and found that the American population's second greatest fear is death. What's the greatest fear? Public speaking. Anybody who's seen me speaking publicly will know I'm more comfortable making a football talk than talking myself. I don't hate it and I'm not scared of it, but as a well-known Indigenous Australian I'm often called upon to offer my thoughts on a variety of topics, and while I'm always willing to give public speaking a go, it's not my area of expertise. I'm a naturally shy person, who doesn't feel completely at home in front of a microphone. That doesn't mean I don't have anything to say, it's just that I prefer to do so in my own time and space, which is the luxury that writing a book provides.

When I was a kid I'd look at autobiographies in the school library. There was *The Greatest: My Own Story* by Muhammad Ali, and *The Art of Fast Bowling* by Dennis Lillee. I couldn't comprehend how somebody could live a life so interesting and exciting that people would want to pay money to read about it. I knew of Ali and Lillee of course, and I knew why they'd become famous, but I found books to be intimidating and the idea of anybody writing a whole one about themselves was just mind-blowing.

Yet here I am, writing my memoir. And here you are, reading it. Thank you. This is the perfect forum for me to tell my tale, because my ancestors have always been storytellers and we've been around since before books, or paper, or ink were invented. Our stories have long been told through the oral tradition, and later, through cave drawings.

Some stories can never be told, because there are other people involved who value their privacy, and without permission I'm not going to betray their trust. My life incorporates as much tragedy as triumph. My time on this earth involves three major phases: before my football career, during my football career and after my football career. How I became a person whom some people view as 'an inspiration' or the 'spokesperson for a generation' when my childhood was spent on an Aboriginal reservation, and my adult existence has been unconventional, is as much a mystery to me as it may be to you. But it did happen and this is how.

A final cultural note: I am completely at ease with myself and my people being referred to as Aboriginal, Indigenous or First Nations, and with new and old terms. All of which are used in the following pages. We've often been rebranded, usually with good intentions, and I imagine there may be further future titles bestowed upon us too. As long as they're attributed in a friendly fashion that's fine by me.

# ONE

I am a proud Noongar man. There are various ways to spell Noongar, including Nyoongar and Nyungah, but this spelling—*Noongar*—is my personal preference.

Noongars are Aboriginal Australian peoples who live in the south-west corner of Western Australia, from Esperance on the south coast to Geraldton on the west coast.

We divide the year into six seasons rather than four. November–December is 'the fruiting'; January–February is 'the hot dry'; March–April is 'first rains, first dew'; May–June is 'the wet'; July–August is 'the cold wet'; September–October is 'the flowering'. Most of these seasonal names determine whether our diets are going to consist of wheat, seeds and fruits, meat from hunting, or fish from the ocean.

There are 14 different Noongar families of Noongar Boodja (meaning Country or land) who speak several dialects. I'm from the Wilman tribe. The colonisation of our people by the British and the genocide that followed took a toll on our population. We saw the people getting off their ships and couldn't comprehend what was occurring. We assumed they were white spirits, the ghosts of our deceased relatives returning, and so we welcomed them ashore with ceremonial song and dance-driven corroborees. When we realised they were claiming our land, we protested. When they began to indiscriminately reduce the number of native animals during random shooting sprees, we took ownership of the livestock they had on board. They perceived the deliberately lit fires of our land-management back-burning process to be an act of hostility towards them.

Our spears were no match for their guns. We died in large numbers. From 1890 to 1960, many of those who survived had their children 'forcibly adopted' by white authorities who wanted to indoctrinate the 'natives' into their religious congregations. The parents of those children were never told where their children had been taken and were left to grieve on their own. The children were often told their parents had died. Those children eventually became known as the Stolen Generations.

Before that, however, we were a thriving and successful national community. Aboriginal life revolves around the family, the community, the tribe, the land and the Dreamtime. None of these elements can exist without the others. From birth, Aboriginal children are taught to show reverence to their elders, who we see as playing a vital leadership role in our lives. Their role is to provide advice, support and wisdom, especially to younger members of the community. These values are the cornerstone of most healthy cultures, but to us they're non-negotiable. Aboriginal people see the land (or Country) as the most important aspect of our spiritual identity. We take pride in the land as it encompasses our history, resilience and survival, as well as providing food and water.

The Dreamtime is like our core religion. The story explains our origins and reminds us of the importance of maintaining the land we're lucky to live on, the people we're lucky to live with, plus the flora and fauna we're lucky to be surrounded by. Dreamtime is how we view the duration and creation of rivers, streams and waterholes, land, plants and animals. One of these spirits is the Rainbow Serpent, named Wagyl. Replace our serpent with your god and I'm sure you get the idea. The main difference is that we gave our creator a lot more than seven days to get the job done. Need some time to rest, bro!

We Noongars are represented in the Australian Football League more than any other Indigenous tribe. It's not a competition but we're proud of how many from our region have made it at the elite level. From Graham 'Polly' Farmer to Lance 'Buddy' Franklin, our numbers continue to grow.

*A warning—to my grandkids especially, if and when you read my book—that the following pages are going to contain some words, phrases and events which might upset or even frighten you. Ask for adult advice or maybe wait until you're a whole lot older before continuing reading. Thank you.*

# TWO

Black cunt.

There were days when I thought that was my name.

Reading those two words is shocking, right? Seeing them in print, seeing them as the first two words in a chapter of somebody's life story? Harsh stuff, I know.

Please don't judge me by the use of the c-word in this chapter, or anywhere else later on. I cannot tolerate it. I don't use it and don't like it when others do so. But it's a part of my story, and the story of my people. From now on I'll water down the impact by using an asterisk.

This chapter might be too much for you. Fair enough. Some of the moments I describe were too much for me too, but I didn't have the option of putting the book down.

Don't get me wrong. This is not a book by *one* blackfella complaining about *all* whitefellas. I don't hate anyone. I love lots of people, and many of them are white. This isn't a book about how hard my life has been either. There have been hard times due to the colour of my skin, which I would not have experienced if I was white. That's just a fact. There have also been hard times caused by my own poor decisions. But mainly I've been privileged to lead a reasonably lucky life, in a reasonably lucky country. Like everybody, I've had my ups and downs. It's just that my ups have been way, way up, and my downs have been way, way down. Many of the highs and lows have played out in public too. I'm not going to shy away from the most well-known moment of my entire life. But, no matter how proud I am of it, I hope that moment doesn't overshadow the rest of my sporting career.

*Black c\*nt.*

Imagine somebody saying those two words straight to your face. And imagine the face those words are coming out of has an angry, ugly expression on it. And usually they'll say it after ten (or ten thousand) other people have already said the same thing, or worse, that same day. This describes many football matches I played in. It came from the crowd a lot more than from my fellow footballers. Sometimes I wouldn't dare chase the footy if it went near the fence, for reasons a whitefella could never know.

At the peak of my AFL football career, in my prime, I hunted the ball like my ancestors hunted kangaroos. I hunted it with intent. For me it's no coincidence that the Sherrin football has a kangaroo logo branded on its hide. For myself and my forebears, catching that kangaroo put food in the mouths of our families. As a kid who chased kangaroos and as an adult who chased a footy, I caught them and I used them well. If I didn't, I wouldn't be able to eat.

I played AFL footy for fun, but I also appreciated receiving an appropriate financial reward. It gave me a level of confidence I never believed I'd be able to achieve in a white man's world. Sometimes the racist insults affected my confidence, which affected my form. That's not a complaint, it's just the truth. To paraphrase the soul singer James Brown, it's as much a *white* world as it is a *man's* world. If you're black, or a woman, you're behind the white man in line. Or you're faced with people belittling your best days by calling you a black c*nt for no reason.

From a young age, I was consistently a very good, often great, player. I can say that with clarity because I'd regularly do stuff on the field that even *I* didn't know I was capable of. Sometimes I wished there was a second me so I could high-five myself! I had my share of poor games where I couldn't find a rhythm. Games when I played with injuries. Games when my opponent beat me fair and square (thanks for nothing, Mil Hanna). But the majority of my career saw me find the ball often enough to make me feel like I'd made a worthy contribution. And on the occasions when the planets aligned for four whole quarters, it was like . . . magic.

On my best days even the most outrageous ideas fell into place exactly the way I'd imagined. Often there was no nerve required and no attempt involved because, at my best, I played footy without thought, allowing my body to absorb my mind's messages and apply those instructions without consulting

13

my consciousness first. The adrenaline rush when I flew like a bird, taking skyscraper marks as I met the football at its highest point. The exhilaration when I'd kick a goal from too great a distance while running at too fast a pace. The deafening roar of elation from the crowd. You know those final euphoric seconds just before an orgasm eventuates, and then the ecstasy of the orgasm itself? Those on-field moments felt as good as that. It's not just me who's able to experience such highs: thousands of other highly skilled athletes worldwide, or even people in non-sporting sectors of society, have experienced supreme moments.

But I'm telling you my story. And part of my story involves wondering what kind of person would deliberately want to ruin the day of somebody they don't even know by saying something that could damage the other person forever? What do those kinds of people get out of stealing someone's sunshine? Like everyone, I want to be loved. Or, at the very least, I do not want to be hated. More than anything, racism just does not make sense. Hating me for the colour of my skin? Imagine hating someone for the colour of their eyes, or the colour of their hair? Ridiculous.

The word 'c*nt' deserves a chapter of its own. A name for a woman's private parts should not be used as an insult towards anybody. The comeback quote where somebody says, 'I'd call him a c*nt but he doesn't have the warmth or the depth' is always a winning response. But, until a major shift in society occurs, let's agree that if you're called a c*nt it is usually intended to be offensive.

What insult would hurt you most? What extra word, placed before the word 'c*nt', directed at you, would most ruin your mood? The first word needs to be demeaning. The first word has to convey something 'less than ideal' in the mind of the antagonist. Imagine doing a job you love—whether it's baking cakes, tinkering under the bonnet of your car, or managing people—and being called the name that would most negatively affect you, every single day. While you were doing your job. A job you were good at. A job you were respected for. A job you enjoyed. And I don't mean when you're called a harsh name in a *friendly* fashion, as men of a certain generation are prone to do. Not like how a mate you're drinking with at a bar would say, 'C'mon, it's your shout, you cheap c*nt.' No, I mean in a way deliberately intended to hurt you. To upset you. To ruin your day. Your week. Maybe your life.

During an English Premier League game between Queens Park Rangers and Chelsea in October 2011, Chelsea defender John Terry allegedly called his opponent Anton Ferdinand a 'fucking black c*nt' on the pitch. The incident ended up in court and an English Football Association disciplinary hearing cost John Terry the England national team's captaincy. While Terry was found not guilty in court, England's FA later found him guilty; he was given a four-match ban and a £220,000 fine. Nine years later Ferdinand agreed to participate in a deeply moving BBC documentary in which he said his decision to remain silent burned a hole inside him. 'I have kicked myself and beat myself up daily, for nearly a decade for not speaking out,' he said.

Some might call him a weak c*nt. Tell him to drink a glass of concrete and harden the fuck up, or whatever other thoughtless phrases people use when attempting to minimise an emotional or psychological pain they don't understand. You know what I'd call Anton Ferdinand? Human. I'd call him a fellow man who started his day hoping it would be a good one, like we all do. Who, in his case, began that day in 2011 on a high because he knew it was the day of the week he got to do what he loved. What he was best at. What he got paid good money to do, and what people paid good money to see him do. He ended that day on a low. That decade on a low. I can't swear to it but it seems that being able to name *the* person who called you *that* name in *the* game suggests it wasn't happening very often in England by then.

Even once is too often, and Anton's pain is palpable, but if I were to name every game in which I was called a black c*nt, and every person who did so, it would fill the remaining pages of this book. I've forgotten more racist insults than I remember. And I remember a lot. What I prefer to remember is the long life I've been privileged to lead.

You might see Aboriginal people spelling the word 'black' without the 'c'. You may have seen it written as 'Blak'. Aboriginal artist, broadcaster and activist Destiny Deacon asked a gallery displaying her artworks back in 1994 if they'd spell the title of her exhibition 'Blakness: Blak City Culture' without the 'c'. The gallery agreed and Destiny described her reasoning like this: 'Growing up Aboriginal, I regularly heard the words "You little black c*nts" from white people. It's still common to have "black c*nts" being shouted at us on the streets,' Deacon said. 'So as a result, my motive was that I just wanted to take the "c" out of "black", and it's been picked up by a lot of my fellow Aboriginals ever since.'

The wonderful award-winning young Aboriginal singer–songwriter Thelma Plum's superb song 'Better In Blak' (from the awesome album of the same name) was nominated for an ARIA and is a song I can directly relate to, because it's about taking personally aimed incidents of racist abuse and turning them into something positive and hopefully progressive.

# THREE

Businesses like to boast about how long it's been since they started. The duration of anything's (or anyone's) existence is often a measure of well-earned respect. Stuff that 'stands the test of time' is most often rewarded. People in the Commonwealth used to receive a letter from the queen on their 100th birthday. Someone who works for the same employer for 50 years will be gifted a gold watch. We trust those who stick around.

The Fortune of War pub, in the Sydney Harbour precinct known as The Rocks, was established in 1828. So they've been around for more than 190 years. That's a lot of beers.

Arnott's began making biscuits in 1865. That's a ton of Tim Tams and a shitload of Savoury Shapes. Akubra started up in 1874. Lots of faces protected from the sun by their hats for more than 140 years.

Indigenous Australians? We've been here for more than 60,000 years. That's 315 times longer than the Fortune of War pub, 375 times longer than Arnott's, and 428 times longer than Akubra. But I wonder if us mob are anywhere near as respected as the pub, the biscuits and the hats? The average Australian's life expectancy is currently 82 years. So you'd have to live your entire lifespan 731 times before you'd been around as long as Indigenous Australians have occupied this land.

My own contribution to our great nation began in the rural Western Australian town of Kellerberrin on 25 September 1965. I was named Neil Elvis Winmar: Neil, after my dad, and Elvis, after, well, a fella who is still remembered long after he left this world.

On the other side of the continent, on the very same day I was born, it was VFL (AFL) Grand Final Day. St Kilda played Essendon at the Melbourne Cricket Ground before 104,846 people. Thirty-two years and two days later, I would play for St Kilda on Grand Final Day at the MCG (after almost being recruited by Essendon).

Kellerberrin is in the wheatbelt region of Western Australia. The town is a two-and-a-half hour, 205-kilometre drive north-east from Perth on the Great Eastern Highway. Thirty kilometres south of Kellerberrin is Kokerbin Rock, said to be Australia's second largest monolith after Uluru.

Kellerberrin is also famous for being the birthplace of three Indigenous boys who went on to play in the AFL. One of those was Derek Kickett, who won the Sandover Medal at Claremont for being the best player in the West Australian Football League

(WAFL) in 1987, before playing a total of 152 games for North Melbourne, Essendon and Sydney in the AFL. With his mop of long curly hair and his Mexican bandit moustache, Kickett's evasive skills and long torpedo punts set the AFL alight. Byron Pickett, who played 204 games for North Melbourne, Port Adelaide and Melbourne, was born in Kellerberrin too. He won the illustrious Norm Smith Medal for best on ground in the 2004 AFL Grand Final (which his team Port Adelaide won). Byron was renowned as one of the toughest players in the game's history, with his hybrid of silky skills and ability to bulldoze through unsuspecting opponents, within the rules.

The other widely known individual born in Kellerberrin is me.

•

My dad was born in a tent under a tree on 1 August 1947 at Quairading, Western Australia. The tent and the tree were considered relatively luxurious conditions. Many Indigenous folk from that era would have killed for a tent *or* a tree. Dad was named Neal with an 'a'. When I was born (in an actual hospital), I was named after my dad but somehow the spelling was Neil with an 'i'. But my name quickly became Nicky—neither me nor any family member remember why.

My mum's name was Meryle. She was born in 1950 at Beverley, Western Australia. Mum's dad, Albert Humphries, was my grandpop. He was a lovely and loving man who was the storyteller in our family, passing on personal and traditional Aboriginal tales through the generations. Nan was Mum's mum, and *her* mum was half Native American, after *her* mum met a crew member of a US whaling ship from Connecticut in the late 1800s, which briefly landed in Western Australia. Nan and Pop used to roll empty drums down to the nearby freshwater source and roll full drums back up again, but then the white farmers took ownership of the region and fenced off our water supply. A lot of Aboriginals went to fight in the war on the promise of a piece of land upon their return but that turned out to be a lie. They were simply cannon fodder. Mum and Dad got married in Doodlakine, Western Australia, and had a baby girl named Robyn, but she died early, before I was born, from a spider bite. My parents never completely recovered from her death. I was born next, followed by my brother Frank, my sister Heather, and another brother Ben (now deceased). Death has been a constant in my life, which has caused me to be constantly running from my own mortality. It can be a lonely way to live but I've mainly been acting on instinct. That's what I tell myself when I can't sleep at night anyway.

Dad was a shearer and Mum looked after us kids, occasionally working as a cleaner to make ends meet. In 1967 Mum and Dad moved to Pingelly in search of work. Pingelly Reserve was a 25-acre area where the white settlers had decided we Indigenous folks had to live. Up to 200 of us lived at the reserve at any one time. We had to fashion our own houses, or dwellings, from corrugated iron sheets. We leaned these against one another to form a makeshift shelter, with no real doors or windows. We boiled in the summer and froze in the winter. We'd often be kept awake by our neighbours four or five shacks away snoring. A couple having an argument, or the opposite, could be heard by most of the reserve.

Most of these shacks had dirt floors but as the years passed some families were lucky enough, or had worked hard enough, to afford concrete. We considered those families 'posh'. It was possible, depending on how much corrugated iron was available, to create 'rooms' within these dwellings, but in reality they were simply separated spaces. Families were often large and so each room housed numerous people, with adults in one space and kids in another. There was no running water, never enough toilet blocks available, and an ancient sewerage system so the aroma of excrement surrounded us at all times. Wild winds and rains rushed through the shaky iron shacks and there was illness everywhere.

The facilities improved a bit when shower blocks were eventually built, but everyone had to wait until the fire underneath the tanks had been lit or else the water was too cold.

Local white residents confined us to the reserve because they didn't want us living among them. All the land as far as the eye could see had previously, for 60,000 years or more, belonged to us. We were happy to share our territory with the white people when they arrived but it wasn't long before they began fencing it off and claiming it as Crown land, leaving us to all live on top of each other in a designated area. We became a dispossessed people. The Western Australian government's official plan to try to appease us, as announced in the late 1950s, was for *transitional housing* at the very edge of town, with gradual integration leading to full assimilation with the white township, but the Pingelly Shire Council had failed to get with the program. Officials would occasionally arrive from Perth, pretending to be concerned and making promises of improvements, but real progress didn't take place until the late sixties, when a national referendum led towards actual change. We'd gone from centuries of living across the length and breadth of this great southern land, to being herded like cattle onto reserves or missions, to living on top of each other in tin sheds. A collective claustrophobia created psychological shackles that restricted and constricted us in every way imaginable.

Until then, life remained grim. In 1967, a Pingelly magistrate named E.O. Lange, when sentencing a 17-year-old Aboriginal boy to six months' detention for stealing lollies and cigarettes, issued a statement to the media: 'No matter what all the do-gooders say in Perth, a whipping is the only punishment the Aboriginals fear. Physical pain is what makes these natives sit up and take notice.'

We also had to obey a white-ordered curfew and any Aboriginal found outside the reserve after six at night faced anything from a beating by police officers, or by random white townsfolk, to a stint in gaol, or all of the above. On the rare occasions when we *were* allowed into town, we had to stick to one side of the street, or else another beating or incarceration was likely.

My people often died this way. I'm speaking of my own childhood now, in the 1970s, but it continues to this day. In 2022, a 15-year-old boy named Cassius Turvey was beaten to death with an iron bar as he walked home from school in Perth with his friends. He was killed in broad daylight, by a white man he'd never met, in what Prime Minister Anthony Albanese described as 'clearly a racially motivated attack'.

I felt, and still feel, constant guilt for having black skin. The psychological trauma of constantly feeling like there was shame about being Aboriginal messed with my heart and my mind. It affected my entire outlook because I knew a lot of white people viewed me as being lesser than them.

Then the laws adjusted to allow us to drink in public, but only in a separate bar to the white people. And when the grog began mixing with the fear, anxiety and anger we were experiencing, it led to behaviours that made the local whites claim they'd been right about us all along, even though lots of white folks got messy on the grog without suffering any sanctions.

Imagine that *every* kid was bullying you at school, and every teacher too, and so was everyone on the street and in playgrounds. Adults, children, people in positions of authority, shopkeepers—everyone, everywhere, all the time. Imagine the real fear of being beaten to death on the street with an iron bar.

Imagine what that does to a person. I didn't have to imagine because it was my reality. Even as an adult it is still extremely difficult to try to undo because it's the only way of living you've ever known.

Then, if you're lucky like me, you find yourself excelling at an endeavour that white people respect and these same people are suddenly wanting to be your friend and acting like you're even more special than *they* are. You should be grateful and relieved, but you're wary and watchful, even of the people who never meant harm and have always been on your side. You can't bring yourself to trust these swiftly adjusted attitudes. You're always wondering what the catch is and so you try to get as much out of these new white friends as you can before it all turns to shit. You get as much money off as many white men as you can, you arrange as many liaisons with adoring white women as you can because you don't expect any of this to last long enough for you to have to answer for any of it.

You're always sceptical of this worship, of being feted for the very same attribute you've been shamed for—your Aboriginality—and you can't believe your troubles are over. You're sure a trick is being played on you and you know that eventually the status quo you've been consigned to your entire life will come roaring back to sit you on your arse and make you feel foolish for daring to believe your life of pain might possibly be over.

You're a fox in the henhouse; you're a bank robber who can hear the sirens getting louder; you're an Aboriginal footy star who white people think is superhuman when all you've known beforehand is that lots of them have been treating you like you're subhuman.

How is anybody supposed to navigate such a monumental shift of their earth's axis, even if it's in their favour? It's like those people below the poverty line who win $80 million on the lottery but all it does is destroy their life because they're not programmed to handle it.

Ten years later you're still playing great football and the adoration continues but you've left a trail of destruction in your wake because you never expected you'd still be alive to have to clean it up. You've failed to foster long-term relationships or adhere to agreements, based on a disbelief that this comparative utopia actually ever existed, or would exist for much longer. You've been living day by day in this white majority society and they've made you feel welcome, but your career has lasted this long and you've still never felt safe enough to put precautions in place. Precautions such as saving money, owning a house, staying married, parenting properly. You ignore a nagging resentment that it took supreme football skills (thus making you a commodity) for previously closed doors to be flung open. You feel for your Indigenous brethren who weren't born with your talent, who never have and maybe never will be afforded the red carpet treatment you've received. You rage internally at the injustice. You sometimes feel like a race-traitor. You envy and admire the fellow Indigenous footballers who have managed to rise above the fear and confusion. You also know that, if not for your sublime ability with a ball, you'd most probably no longer be here on this earth. You'd have succumbed to depression, mental illness or physical ailments.

You're aware that if your skin was white, none of these thoughts would have ever crossed your mind, let alone tormented you for a lifetime. But you bury the bewildered thoughts and you control the chaotic emotions and you smile for selfies, dozens of them a day, and you embrace the wellwishers, because these people are excited to see you and that's *something*, right? They're being kind, isn't that what you wanted? You're somebody. The only question is . . . who?

Maybe my self-assessment is accurate. Or maybe I was an arsehole.

•

Back on the reservation our parents enforced the curfew more than the law did. They were constantly telling us, 'Don't think you're being naughty or cheeky or funny by disobeying the rules. You'll get locked up or stolen or maybe something much worse.' These weren't idle threats. These consequences were realities. It was a hideous way for us all to live, but what choice did we have? We'd been rounded up like livestock into a fenced-off yard. On the reservation there was a makeshift kindergarten, school and town hall. My aunty was a teacher at the school so Mum and Dad always found out if I misbehaved.

Nobody had much money so we'd often need to be inventive if we wanted to eat. We'd build home-made rabbit traps. We'd herd kangaroos into barbed wire fences and the biggest kid in the group would have to knock the roo on the head with a branch until it was dead. One big whack would usually do it, putting it out of its misery. We'd catch goannas if we could. Goannas are basically the last of the dinosaurs so survival is their strongest skill. Even if you were sure they were dead you'd have to break their legs before you cooked them on the fire, otherwise they'd sometimes just stand up and run away. That was a lesson my aunty learned the hard way. Before that day, I thought it was only in old-fashioned movies where ladies fainted.

We didn't *like* this way of living but it didn't worry us either. It was simply our way of life.

# FOUR

Dad was a genuine Australian Rules Football pioneer because he helped form the first ever All Aboriginal football team. The Great Southern League in our area had a rule that only allowed three Aboriginal players per team. This severely restricted opportunities for local Noongar footballers. Coach Des Little knew there was an abundance of talented Aboriginal players who couldn't squeeze into the white teams three at a time, so the obvious solution was to create an all-black team. And so, in 1967, Dad became an original member of the Pingelly Tigers, an All-Aboriginal team with Des as the coach.

The players from that Tigers team were Aussie Rules royalty, going by the names Jetta, Hill, Abraham, Narkle, Ugle, Sampi, Kickett, Bennell and many others, including the Collards, who were famous in Western Australia, and of course Winmar. Many descendants of these pioneers have played for numerous

AFL teams, leaving an immeasurable legacy to the game. In 2022, at the age of 89, coach Des Little was honoured with a NAIDOC Award for 'allowing Aboriginal people to fulfil their dreams'.

The Tigers players often travelled 200 kilometres to play each week. It gave them a sense of purpose. A lot of teams refused to play if my dad was picked, because they said his rough and ready style of play, in which he'd let nobody stand in his way or tolerate racism on any level, was a risk they weren't willing to take. Dad often came home covered in the scent of Old Spice or Brut 33, which he'd borrowed from a team-mate in the rooms after a post-game shower. That usually happened after a win. Mum would smile and blush as he walked in the door with a spring in his step, after which we'd soon get sent to Aunty's for the night.

Around that time I was excited to start school, especially as I knew most of the kids who'd be going there with me. But once school started, the classroom was my least preferred place to spend the day, especially if one of the various religious groups who visited us had been allowed into class on a recruiting drive.

In the playground, 'kiss chasey' was a popular game. I was an enthusiastic participant, even though I mainly ran around on my own. I'm not sure if that's because I was unappealing or because I was so competitive I wouldn't let anyone catch me. I had a crush on two girls but neither of them seemed to know I existed, maybe because I'd run so far away they didn't know I was there.

I loved the library as it was a quiet space away from the mayhem in the yard.

One of my teachers was Mark Brennan, whose brother Michael Brennan would later become a two-time premiership player with the West Coast Eagles. Mark saw straight away that I could play footy and was a skilled kick on my right foot, so he set about teaching me to kick on my left foot too. He knew I had great running endurance due to the countless kiss chasey miles he'd seen me fruitlessly compiling. It's a lot harder for the opposition to stop you if they never know which foot you're going to kick with, and all the hard work I did on improving those both-sides-of-the-body skills became a great advantage for me throughout my career.

•

In 1975, when I was ten, I snuck into the first film ever shown at the Pingelly drive-in. I didn't so much sneak in as jump out of my bedroom window and climb a tree near the drive-in fence with a mate, where we watched from forks in the branches, the smell of popcorn from the kiosk filling the air. The movie was a French softcore porn film called *Emmanuelle*. I'll never forget the movie's promo poster, because it said—'Emmanuelle. She's sensual, but she's elegant. She's fantasy, but she's fun.'

Back then Pingelly's broader population was barely 1500 people but I can assure you that every adult in town—white and black—was at that drive-in for the first screening of *Emmanuelle*.

There were panel vans everywhere, some with those classic stickers that read 'If this van's rockin', don't bother knockin''.

A lot of the audience had to walk home from the drive-in that night because there were so many sex scenes (not that I really understood what was happening during those scenes at the time) that all the tooting of horns and flashing of headlights caused a lot of car batteries to go flat. I made sure I ran home as fast as I could because Mum and Dad were at the drive-in too and I was supposed to be home in bed.

In later years, the morning after a drive-in movie night I'd usually ask my parents about the movie they'd gone to see, but that morning we all just ate our cornflakes without saying a word.

The first drive-in movie we saw as a family was a re-run of *The Good, The Bad and The Ugly*, but we spent the whole movie arguing about which of us best fit each of the three descriptions.

That year turned out to be quite eventful as it was also when Mum and Dad bought a TV. The day they brought that little black and white TV set home was one I will never forget.

By this time my parents had managed to move into an actual house, just outside the reservation. Sure, it was small, but we had real walls and windows. But the cherry on top was the TV, which made us feel like we were wealthy.

My favourite show was *The Winners* on Sunday nights on the ABC, hosted by Drew Morphett, where they showed selected highlights of that weekend's VFL games. We often watched *Countdown* directly before that, with Sherbet and Skyhooks seemingly on with a new hit song every week.

In 1975 North Melbourne won their first ever premiership, more than 100 years after being founded. They continued this run, winning the premiership in 1977 as well, and since they were playing the best football at the time, they were featured on *The Winners* a lot. Their supremacy and possibly the fact that they were called the kangaroos (hundreds of which roamed around Pingelly, trying to avoid becoming our dinner) saw me become a North Melbourne supporter. Kind of. It was more like all my favourite players played for North. I loved Stan Alves (who would later become my coach), Ross Glendinning (who I knew was from Western Australia), Wayne Schimmelbusch and the superstar Malcolm Blight. But my absolute idol was Keith Greig, the pale-faced winger who seemed to float on air. Knowing Keith Greig had won back-to-back Brownlow Medals (awarded to the VFL/AFL's best and fairest player at the end of each season) in 1973–74 only added to my hero worship. With the iconic Ron Barassi as their coach, North made four grand finals in a row. After beating Hawthorn by ten goals in 1975 (the year we got our TV), they lost to Hawthorn in 1976, then won against Collingwood in 1977 (after the game had been a draw the week before, in what was the first grand final to be televised in colour), then lost to Hawthorn in 1978. I loved seeing Yorta Yorta man Glenn James umpire a lot of the games on TV, because I'd never seen a black man policing white men before.

Most Mondays, after watching *The Winners*, my brothers and I, along with any mates nearby, would go outside and try to replicate the best marks and goals we'd watched the night before. We ripped the bench seat out of an old EK Holden so we could spring off it as we jumped onto each other's backs to take spectacular marks. Or we'd chop down a tree and jump off the stump. We were pretty wild but it was a terrific training regime. It often became competitive so some kids (including me) would head home with bloodied noses or split lips and think nothing of it.

We'd also pretend each other's front yards were Victorian teams' home grounds we'd seen on TV: the MCG, Princes Park, the Junction Oval, Arden Street and the Lake Oval. One time we tried to re-create the mysteriously permanent mud at St Kilda's home ground in Moorabbin by tipping buckets of water (and using our new hose) on the dirt outside but Mum cracked the shits because of the mess we traipsed inside. We blocked the shower drain at my aunty's house once, flooding the bathroom, and she almost killed us. A lot of the time I'd avoid being disciplined by Mum and Dad (or my aunty) because I'd run so fast they couldn't catch me, and then by the time I came back they'd have calmed down.

It was only later that I realised the hose and the buckets helped teach me how to handle a heavy, wet footy, which would be important when I began playing in the more wintry Victorian weather.

•

With only the grassy areas within the reservation to occupy our time, us kids were usually going stir-crazy so Mum and

Dad scrounged up enough money to buy a second-hand Mini Minor so we could get out more. One time we drove to Narrows Bridge in Perth. It was just a massive bridge but that was exciting enough for us. A fireworks display was going to be on that night so our plan was to sit by the Swan River, which we call Bilya, and watch. Even without the fireworks we'd have been happy just to look at the sheer size of the Swan River itself. We also took pleasure in simply looking at the bridge's scale and architecture while marvelling at the incredible amount of traffic. Looking didn't cost a thing, after all.

Not only did our family now own a car but it also had a working radio in it, which was always tuned to an ABC station my parents loved that played mainly country music. It was November, it was stinking hot, and with no such thing as air-conditioning in cars (or in our car anyway), we were hanging our heads out the windows the whole way there and back, hot wind in our hair, sharing a crisp apple between us, singing along to 'Your Cheatin' Heart' and 'I'm So Lonesome I Could Cry' by Hank Williams, 'I Walk the Line' and 'Ring Of Fire' by Johnny Cash, or anything by Merle Haggard, Jim Reeves and Charley Pride. If Mum had a choice she usually went with Patsy Cline's big hits like 'I Fall To Pieces', 'Walkin' After Midnight' and 'Back in Baby's Arms', all of which I can still sing word for word. Sometimes even more modern stuff might be playing, such as Blondie. Mum loved 'Heart of Glass' especially. My brother Frank loved The Beatles and only The Beatles. I liked them too but there's a limit. I spent a lot of time wishing Frank himself lived in a yellow bloody submarine.

For me, above all else, then and forever, it was Elvis Presley. From my childhood until my dying day, I'll always believe a house or a car is not the same unless you've got Elvis in it.

If we'd been good kids on a road trip, we'd get treated to a Wagon Wheel, a White Knight chocolate bar or a packet of Cobbers for the drive back. Those were the days we'd always remember.

Much later that night, back at home after the Narrows Bridge adventure, I was briefly awoken by my head bumping into the front door frame as Mum carried my sleepy little self out of the car and into bed. Whenever that happened she'd tearfully apologise and I'd say, 'That's all right, Mama.'

•

My first proper game of footy was with the Pingelly Under 12s, known as D Grade. Every kid just chased the ball around for the whole game, nobody bothering about playing in their positions. In recent times, at AFL level, this kind of playing style has been called a 'rolling maul', which caused rules to be adjusted because it's ugly to watch. But as a kid all I remember is how fantastic it felt to be playing in an organised game, with matching team jumpers, actual goalposts instead of designated trees or jumpers placed on the ground, and umpires with real whistles, plus a canteen to buy a potato cake afterwards.

I got my hands on the ball a fair bit most games and generally had fun. We all did. We were ten or eleven, so having fun was our job. Mum didn't have fun though. She'd go through a box of tissues during each game, crying with the fear of me getting hurt. I always knew Mum would cook up my much-loved roast lamb with lots of gravy after a game to reward me for surviving. Dad dished out the discipline at home, but Mum had the soft touch. If she was baking a cake and I'd been a good boy, she'd let me lick the beaters. Her cooking was the best, not only nourishing her family but expressing her love and keeping the peace.

Dad was a footy fanatic and saw how quickly and skilfully I was picking up every aspect of the game. We became a two-man team, with Dad helping me to become as proficient as possible in all areas, by making himself available as often as possible and coaching me to the best of his ability.

When I was 13, Dad found a working portable record player down the tip and I bought my first ever vinyl single: 'Up There Cazaly' by Mike Brady. Years later I became aware that the song was originally commissioned by Channel Seven as a 60-second TV commercial to promote the footy broadcasts. It exploded and was swiftly extended into a full song. Brady had been offered the job due to his success with advertising jingles, such as Hard Yakka, SPC Baked Beans and Spaghetti, and You Can't Beat a SAO for a Snack. My mates and I loved the final lines of 'Up There Cazaly' and would repeat those final words about the crowd being on our side at the top of our lungs.

I played a bit of cricket too, mainly with a tennis ball that had one side taped up, so that it would swing. But I lost interest pretty quickly the first time we played with a real cricket ball. Playing against my brothers and other boys from the reserve, we tended to be aggressive so bouncers bowled at the head were commonplace, and with Western Australia almost permanently bathed in sunshine, the ball would come rocketing off hard baked surfaces at a frightening pace. If you've ever wondered why a lot of Western Australian cricketers play the hook shot so well, it's because they've had more practice. For me, having a rock-hard missile flying at 100 kilometres an hour towards my face on a regular basis was alarming. I once soiled my slacks after barely dodging a short-pitched delivery and to this day I forgive myself without question.

Despite my aversion to cricket, one of my best mates was a kid named Geoff Marsh. We shared a desk at school. The rest of us had Kmart brand bats at best (often we'd have to make do with a fence paling) but Geoff's bat was a Gray-Nicolls with an actual rubber grip. Geoff played five games of footy for South Fremantle's senior side before committing himself to cricket, and went on to play 50 Test matches as an opening batsman for Australia, alongside David Boon and later Mark Taylor. To me, however, Geoff'll always be the kid who could make fart sounds with his hand shoved into his armpit.

I was a little better at basketball than I was at cricket but didn't enjoy the fact that you couldn't kick the ball. As a swimmer I made a good rock.

After our junior footy games finished I'd go watch Dad and my uncles play in their senior games, getting there as early as I could to ensure I got the job of working the manual scoreboard, because payment for that task was a can of Coke and a Polly Waffle, luxuries we were rarely able to afford.

Our family was still at the stage where Mum and Dad would occasionally encourage us kids to jump nearby farmers' fences and sneakily catch yabbies from their dams for dinner (if we'd failed to catch a kangaroo or a goanna) or steal oranges from their trees. The word 'nearby' in Western Australian can mean '5 miles', so for my next birthday Dad gave me my first bike, a dragster with a huge back wheel and a tiny front wheel, which he'd found at the tip. Having my own transport widened my world tremendously.

# FIVE

My high school was literally across the road from Pingelly Primary School. The major difference was that at high school they could give you the cane. It's hard to imagine nowadays that teachers were allowed to hit kids as hard as they could with a wooden cane, but they did and I copped my fair share. The worst was when I got blamed for breaking a bunch of lockers when it genuinely wasn't me who did it. I didn't want to dob anyone in (I'm tempted to do so right now but will maintain my lengthy loyal silence.) I shut up and tried not to scream. I'd been in trouble for lesser stuff (which I did do) and the locker incident was the final straw from the school's perspective so I got expelled. Luckily for me the expulsion took place the day after our Lord and Saviour Elvis Presley died, so Mum and Dad didn't seem to be as upset about my news as I'd expected. I suspect Mum barely heard my announcement anyway, due to playing Elvis's gospel version of 'Amazing Grace' at full volume about a thousand times in a row. If ever you feel like a cry, give it a go.

Narrogin High School was my next stop, 40 kilometres away on the bus, and 40 kilometres back. I shared a desk with a boy whose mum could afford chicken Twisties but he never gave me any so we couldn't be friends. Plus, the white patches on his face from where the Oxy 10 pimple cream had dried out made me feel squeamish.

I didn't get in trouble there but I didn't know any of the other kids and didn't like the teachers, so after a couple of years I spoke to Dad and we agreed a job with the shire council might be a better bet. I loved and respected Mum but it was Dad who I worshipped and none of my decisions occurred without him.

That shire council job was shearing sheep, which I began to do at the age of 14. I've often heard people say, when speaking about how shitty they think their job is, 'Well, it beats digging holes.' I can tell you that I've done some time digging holes and, well, it beats shearing sheep. Nobody can tell me they know what a really hard day's work is until they've sheared a shitload of sheep in one whack.

Here's what it involves.

I start by grabbing a single sheep firmly but carefully under the jaw, then I turn its head to the side and back a bit, so it's positioned like a dog that's trying to bite a hard-to-reach flea behind its ear. I then turn the sheep's whole body on its side and lift the bugger back up like it's a person sitting on the floor on their bum, with their legs spread out in front of them. The sheep's 'arms', or forelegs, are bent at the elbow, and both its 'hands', or cloven hooves, are held up with my own spare hand. The sheep's spine is upright and leaning between my slightly splayed legs. I'm standing up behind it and bending over forwards, in an awkward, uncomfortable position, but this is the only way to get shearing done. It's a physically demanding and highly skilled job. It has been calculated that shearers use 80 per cent more energy per day than a competitor in the Tour de France.

During my later football career, I didn't study or do an apprenticeship, or accept any of the various offers made by countless companies (usually owned by wealthy and influential Saints supporters) to be trained in numerous industries, so at times I've had no choice since quitting footy but to return to those same shearing sheds.

When you're young and dumb and full of . . . fun, the future unfolds no further than Friday. I think most young people are the same. This short-sightedness is especially rife among sports stars because you're doing what you love, and have always loved, and it seems like life is a piece of piss. Sure, sports stars work hard to reach the top, and then they work even harder to stay there, but it doesn't seem like 'work' at the time.

Shearing doesn't seem like work either. It seems like punishment. Like you've been sentenced to hard labour. Funny that, because it *is* hard labour. You experience not just exhaustion but accumulated deep fatigue. I've seen shearers fall asleep standing up at the bar, beer glass lifted halfway to their mouth, as if they're suddenly frozen in time. They'll then be carried to a couch or a bed somewhere, only to wake up the next morning, fully dressed, with a dick and balls drawn on their forehead. Shearers aren't sophisticated, and never claimed to be, but a tougher breed of worker would be hard to find.

A year's worth of shearing toughened me up in ways that regular sessions in the gym never could. So when I first played for the A Grade Pingelly Panthers senior team at the tender age of 15—after it became obvious to anyone watching on that I was an exceptionally long way ahead of my peers in the junior ranks—I was more prepared than most kids my age to play against fully grown men. A gauge of how swiftly I acclimatised is that I won the best and fairest award in my first season. When they called out my name at the awards night, and handed me that golden trophy, it may as well have been the actual Holy Grail. Mum almost squeezed the life out of me as she hugged me so hard I thought I might actually die, and it was only involuntarily inhaling the heavily applied Charlie eau de toilette spray she'd bought from Revlon to wear on special occasions that revived me.

The reason I didn't get hurt by the monsters I was playing against was the same reason I avoided too much trouble at home—nobody could catch me.

Except for one occasion, when, in the process of dodging and weaving one much older, heavier, more muscular opponent, who I was also probably unintentionally humiliating, I doubled back from one of his approaching team-mates and headed straight back into his path, and he made me pay. He had to really, if he wanted to save face. I got flattened, almost literally, like when Wile E Coyote gets run over by a steamroller in the *Road Runner* cartoons and has to be peeled off the road. My jaw still clicks from that hit.

•

In 1982 every Aboriginal boy in Western Australia was given the biggest confidence boost of our lives. Especially us Noongar kids. Two years earlier every Aboriginal girl had been inspired by Evonne Goolagong Cawley winning her second Wimbledon singles title (during that same era Evonne won the Australian Open four times, the French Open once and was runner-up for four consecutive years at the US Open, all after learning to play as a child with a little racquet cut from the wooden slats of a fruit box). Us footy-mad boys, however, were inspired by Jim and Phil Krakouer from Mount Barker, 400 kilometres from Perth, both being recruited by North Melbourne from Claremont's WAFL team, and immediately setting the VFL alight. We'd seen Aboriginal boys playing VFL before, but nothing like the 'Krakouer Magic' as the two brothers displayed what appeared to be a telepathic understanding, which had helped Claremont to a premiership in 1981.

Jim was the elder brother and among the toughest goal-kicking midfielders to ever play the game. Phil, with his unorthodox yet extremely effective kicking style, was more of an elusive goal-kicking half-forward. They were both electrifying and unstoppable game-changers, together or apart, and they inspired me to believe that playing VFL football was a genuine possibility.

People forget how fast the brothers chased and how hard they tackled when the opposition had the ball. They reminded me of my uncles Barry and Phillip Winmar, who displayed the same traits for our local team back in Pingelly, and it's why I valued chasing and tackling in my own game as much as the more attention-grabbing skills. Not that I had a choice because Dad used to make me and my brother Frank chase the sheep in the paddock at least once a week for an hour or two as tackling practice.

The other aspect of Jimmy Krakouer that us young Aboriginal boys quickly became aware of was that he was regularly getting suspended for dropping his direct opponents like a sack of spuds, and we suspected it may have been a retaliation for racist remarks. For a man of just 67 kilograms, standing at 167 centimetres, Jimmy was incredibly strong. The man's hands were lightning fast and I'm sure if he'd have taken up boxing he'd have made a good fist of that too. Years later, in 1990, I was lucky enough to play alongside him when he joined the Saints, by which time he'd lost a yard of pace but made up for it with crafty cunning. Maybe you can't teach an old dog new tricks but at St Kilda Jimmy proved that his hard-earned old tricks remained worthy.

In 1982, the year the Krakouers first took the VFL competition by the scruff of the neck, South Fremantle's Maurice Rioli (fresh from winning two Simpson Medals for consecutive best on ground performances in WAFL grand finals) made his debut for Richmond and won the Norm Smith Medal for best on ground in the 1982 VFL Grand Final. The Krakouers, in their own debut VFL season, dragged North Melbourne into the 1982 Finals and helped North defeat Essendon in the elimination final before being beaten by Hawthorn in the first semifinal.

Meanwhile, back at Pingelly we lost the A Grade Grand Final, but it wasn't hard to see that me and my mob were starting to make waves, which was further emphasised that same September when my family switched *Countdown* on and saw a band called Goanna perform their song 'Solid Rock' on TV for the first time. Well, we heard them perform the song before we saw it because the only thing onscreen at the beginning was a huge backdrop of Uluru, as that now famous didgeridoo riff, the first of its kind ever heard on commercial radio, kicked in. And sure, the song wasn't by our people—the band was full of white folks—but the song was about our people, our 'sacred land' and it was a first. We were thrilled.

I wrote down the lyrics, and I was amazed at how much extra resonance a song can have when you read the words on paper, separate to hearing them sung to a beat.

Shane Howard, who wrote 'Solid Rock', says the song's inspiration came on a ten-day camping trip at Uluru in 1980. Shane said he experienced an incredible injustice that needed to be dealt with. 'I had to reassess my whole relationship with the land and the landscape, and understand that we had come from somewhere else, and we had disempowered a whole race of people when we arrived.'

# SIX

When West Australian footy legend Mal Brown came to watch the Pingelly Panthers in 1982, I couldn't believe this famous player turned coach (with what I quickly discovered was a powerful personality) had actually rocked up at our local bush footy oval. Not for a second did I think he'd come along to see *me*, who weighed less than a wet flannel.

Mal Brown had played 14 games in the VFL for Richmond in 1974 (kicking 25 goals as a midfielder) but had missed playing in the Tigers premiership that year because he'd been suspended for throwing the ball at an umpire. Mal was a former Sandover medallist for East Perth in 1969, and as captain–coach he'd led East Perth to the premiership in 1972. A month later he led that same team in a game against VFL champions Carlton in what was called the 'Championship of Australia', where the recently crowned premiership teams from

Victoria, South Australia, Western Australian and Tasmania battled it out. The concept didn't last long. It lasted long enough, however, for Big Mal to deliver an unforgettable and regularly replayed moment in which he decided to fight the entire Carlton team by himself, and won!

Mal had been appointed coach of South Fremantle in 1978 and led the club to a WAFL premiership in 1980. Two years later he heard word that one of my team-mates was playing well for the Pingelly seniors so he came to take a look for himself.

I was right about Mal not coming to see me, but at half-time Big Mal came into the rooms, having completely forgotten about the player he'd specifically come to see, told me he'd seen enough to know that I had what he termed 'explosive potential' and made me an offer to play for South Fremantle on the spot.

I waited until Dad drove me home before I told him. Truth was it was a scary proposition. From Pingelly, Perth may as well have been as far away as Pakistan.

'What should I do, Dad?' I asked him.

Dad then spoke a sentence that was like the answer to an equation. 'This is what I prepared you for,' he said.

We hugged hard.

I joined South Fremantle the following year, 1983, having just turned 17.

On the day we met, Mal Brown told me he liked recruiting kids who'd been competing against hardened adults, because he knew they wouldn't be shell-shocked in the big smoke. Not *on* the field anyway. He also knew I'd need support when dealing with racism so the motto he made his South Fremantle players live by was 'If he hits you, he hits me'. Kind of a 'one in, all in' mantra that meant I wouldn't be alone if it got willing out on the ground. In an era when most WAFL teams had a couple of Aboriginal boys in their best team, Mal would select half-a-dozen of us every week.

A pre-season article in a publication named *Westside Football*, titled 'Who's Who in Western Australia', described me as 'A clever little player with fine ball skills. Has a big career in front of him.' Mum bought 40 copies.

For the first eight games I toiled away in the seconds.

Then, on Thursday, 26 May 1983, Mal told me after training that I'd been picked to make my senior debut. It was Round 9 and we were set to play against West Perth at Subiaco Oval on Saturday 28 May. West Perth were known as the Falcons and were coached by Dennis Cometti (who had played 40 games for them many years earlier and has since gone on to become arguably the most popular footy commentator of all time, even if the special Bruce McAvaney might beg to differ).

I called Mum and Dad, we all cried on the phone, and they set about driving the 160 kilometres to witness my big day. My wildest dreams were starting to take shape.

On the day, wearing the number 6, I could barely believe the calibre of the team-mates I lined up alongside. Stephen Michael is considered by many West Australians to be perhaps the greatest footballer to ever pull on a boot. Highly decorated, he was an agile Indigenous ruckman who'd won every possible award before being named captain for my first year at the club. Bruce Monteath was playing his third year back in the WAFL after five years at Richmond where he'd captained the Tigers to the 1980 premiership. Brad Hardie was two years away from joining Footscray in Victoria, where he would win the 1985 Brownlow Medal in his first season. Veteran Noel Carter had played in the Richmond premiership team of 1973, and my fellow blackfella Benny Vigona was one of the most brilliant rovers I'd ever seen. I felt daunted running out for my debut among such esteemed footballers.

The main thing I recall about that first game was the brand-new ball, which I must have got my hands on enough to warrant a second game in Round 10, where, against East Fremantle, I kicked three goals in the final quarter to help us win by just one point. Later that night I watched the replay and heard the commentators say, 'That's a brilliant burst of football by Nicky Winmar, from Pingelly, playing in only his second league game. Winmar has kicked two goals in a row for South Fremantle, making it three from him in this final quarter, to put South Fremantle in front. Great pressure football by Nicky Winmar, a star of the future.'

While it might seem big-headed of me to repeat that early praise, it was much needed for me at the time because I was finding it difficult to comprehend how I possibly had a role to play in the thriving metropolis of Perth. Coming to South Fremantle from Pingelly was like Crocodile Dundee lobbing into New York City. South Freo's population itself was 22,000 compared to Pingelly's 1500, and the greater Perth population was nearly a million people. The first time I went to a shopping mall I felt like Charlie in the chocolate factory.

All these shiny goods and services. All these people spending money on stuff I'd never seen. Like a jaffle maker and soap-on-a-rope. And what about the escalators in those malls! A moving stairwell? Getting into an elevator felt like jumping out of a plane without a parachute. I mean, the doors close when you're in one place, then when they open up you're in a different place? It was like witchcraft. Just the collective noise all those people made freaked me out, as did the sight and sound of the traffic. As for trying to navigate public transport, seriously, who knew what to do?

Perth made me feel insignificant, but seeing and hearing my name in print and on TV made me feel like there was a reason for me to be there.

It also proved to be beneficial for my footy because, after surviving yet another week in the unfamiliar and uncomfortable surroundings of the big city, stepping onto the footy field on a Saturday was like being at home. I was in my comfort zone, a place where I knew I belonged. I played 13 games in that first season, mainly on a wing or at half-forward.

Every week for that first year, I'd somehow find my way back home to Pingelly because I missed Mum's cooking (her lamb's tails cooked in ashes were exquisite), Dad's face-to-face feedback after each game and my siblings. I didn't like or understand the city life. But each week, Dad would take me back, or South Freo would send someone to get me, and away we'd go again.

Sometimes when Dad took me back, Mum would come for the ride, but she always burst into tears when she saw how hard the team trained. She was sure I was going to get hurt, just preparing to play, the same way she'd worried about me when I was playing in the Under 12s. In order to help me fit in, South Freo employed me as a part-time cleaner, wiping down seats and sweeping the grandstand before and after games. I escaped that role as soon as I started getting picked for the senior team, but not before I'd pocketed a handy amount of loose change each week from underneath the seats. I used the money to buy a bottle of Brandavino to drink on the sly with my cousin and neither of us have ever been so sick since.

At the end of that debut South Fremantle season I went on my first footy trip away, and flew in my first aeroplane. If the escalators at Perth shopping malls confused me, how do you reckon I went catching a flight? Somehow my digestive system survived the 700 packets of free peanuts and the gallons of free concentrated orange juice, although the view of the tiny toy houses below did make my stomach feel squiffy.

Hong Kong was our destination. Kowloon made Perth seem like a windswept desert. I was only 17 and couldn't handle any aspect of it, especially all the women, hundreds of women, all stinking of super-strong cheap perfume, grabbing my arm and trying to physically pull me into doorways, offering to love me long time, and offering other stuff that made me tearful and fearful to even hear. The area's exhaust fumes and perfume made me feel like I was going to pass out. The whole sordid environment frightened the fuck out of me (literally). I wasn't old enough to drive, I wasn't old enough to drink, I just wasn't old enough.

I barely left my room after that first foray onto the streets, and instead I watched TV in bed while ignoring a million knocks on the door from my team-mates, insisting I come get wasted with them at the Ned Kelly's Last Stand bar. That overseas footy trip freaked me out so badly I never went on another one, with any team, anywhere, ever again. The best bit was trying to watch *Hogan's Heroes* in Cantonese. I'll never forget that every time Sergeant Schultz said his catchphrase, 'I know nothing!', it sounded like he was saying 'Not yet Mozart see!', which made it somehow even funnier than usual.

I got my driver's licence in October that year, a week after my 18th birthday. South Freo helped me buy a 1976 Cortina four-door. If the dragster bike Dad found at the tip had broadened my horizons, being able to drive as far as I wanted, whenever I wanted, made me feel like an astronaut discovering new planets. That Cortina will always have a place in my heart.

•

During the training sessions for South Freo throughout the summer of 1985–86 we had songs playing over the ground's public address system to help make the hard work in the heat more tolerable. The Warumpi Band's song 'Blackfella/ Whitefella' was easily the most requested by all of us players, no matter our skin colour. I swear I was running faster and kicking longer while it played.

A couple of years later, the magnificent friends-to-the-blackfella, Midnight Oil, released Warumpi's 'Blackfella/ Whitefella' on their Powderworks record label and toured with Warumpi (and support band Gondwanaland) across remote Aboriginal communities. I was lucky enough to catch that tour, and the concert I saw was sensational. It was maybe the first and only time I'd seen the black audience outnumber the white. We all united to dance and sing together under the stars in what was a true cultural crossover, with tangible communal reverence for the song's lyrics. Two years later the Oils released 'Beds Are Burning' which was a huge hit internationally and reminded the world of the issues facing Aboriginal Australians.

Dan Sultan, the masterful Indigenous singer–songwriter (who's been known to wear a St Kilda jumper on stage, which he kindly lifts so he can point to his skin colour at the end of his show, a gesture I am grateful for), told Andrew Stafford at *The Guardian*, 'In this country, we're spoilt for frontpeople [but] Warumpi Band's George Rrurrambu Burarrawanga is the best frontman Australia has ever produced, regardless of how many people, or more to the point how many people don't know it.' Us Aboriginals already loved the many popular songs the Oils had released, especially the ones that spoke directly about our own lives, but nothing that night could top the moment Warumpi performed 'BlackFella/Whitefella'. The response from the audience was almost evangelical.

# SEVEN

In 1986 I missed 13 games with a groin injury, which may have led to my being overlooked for the West Coast Eagles squad, which was named that year in advance of them entering the VFL. I'd been named in the initial squad of 35 but when they were told to cut it back to 30 I missed out.

One night while I was training for South Freo, I was approached and told Essendon's coach Kevin Sheedy wanted to meet me for a coffee. I'd have rather had a beer but was smart enough (just) not to say so. Kevin asked about my ambitions, my education, whether I drank booze or smoked darts. I looked him in the eye and assured him I was a clean-living kid. Which wasn't true. But was it really a lie? Either way, I never heard from him again.

When it comes to how the St Kilda Football Club ended up recruiting me, not even I'm sure what the facts are.

St Kilda's coach in 1986, the year before I arrived, was Graeme Gellie, who had joined the club as a rover from Ballarat in 1978. His debut season in the big league saw him record more handballs than any other player in the competition, *and* he won the Saints' best and fairest award, ahead of famous team-mates such as Trevor Barker and Carl Ditterich. In his first year!

Graeme did his knee before the next season and only eked out another 12 games over the following three years before retiring in 1983. He stayed on as senior coach of the Saints for three years and then agreed to stay on in any capacity the club required. What St Kilda required was somebody to come across to Western Australia and sign me up. I'll let Graeme take it over from here . . .

### Graeme Gellie on Nicky Winmar

In 1983, St Kilda recruiting officer Stuart Trott (who'd played 159 games for the Saints and 41 with the Hawks), was sent to Perth to check out a young talent to whom the Saints' then general manager, triple Brownlow medallist Ian Stewart, had been alerted. The match was between Swan Districts and South Fremantle. It was Stephen Michael's 200th game for Swans, and the prospect in question was Phil Narkle (later to play 48 solid games for the Saints, wearing the largest helmet the game has ever seen). Stuart got to the game early and saw the second half of the reserves game, where he was instantly captivated by a slender 17-year-old named Winmar. As Stuart himself recalled, 'After the seniors game I asked South

Freo coach Mal Brown why the Winmar kid was playing in the seconds and he told me he'd been demoted for a week due to ill-discipline. During the seniors game I observed that Narkle, if he had the ball given to him, was devastating. But this kid Winmar in the twos could get his own ball and then use it with precision under pressure. I found a payphone, called Stewie and told him the Narkle bloke was great and we should get him, but how do we snaffle this kid Winmar while we're at it?'

Narkle was recruited for the following season but Winmar was deemed too raw and inconsistent. Former St Kilda full-forward George Young (108 games, 284 goals) had returned to his home state of Western Australia and become a voluntary talent-spotter for the club. He called St Kilda at the back end of 1986 to say, 'You better send somebody over here and fly this sensational kid named Nicky Winmar to Victoria before someone else gets him.' Nicky, still contracted to South Fremantle, was already on our radar via Stuart Trott's earlier assessment and was now into his fourth season, so I got the job to fly over and bring him back with me as soon as possible.

One of the first hiccups I faced was that Nicky, like all the Indigenous boys, viewed any money he made, and anything he bought with that money, to be equally earned and owned by his relatives and his mates. It was a 'what's mine is yours and what's yours is mine' sort of perspective. A lot of the Indigenous bush families relied on the income their kids might bring in from sheep-shearing or any other kind of work. So if their boy was invited to play footy elsewhere, it stood to reason he'd send the majority of that footy money back home. Or cars he'd bought with that money back home, or TVs, stereos, whatever. The WAFL teams were so keen to please their star Indigenous recruits that they'd regularly advance them their player payments, but trying to solve one problem created another because these young kids became overdrawn and plunged into debt. A gentleman named Harold Harper was the football manager of South Fremantle and he was accustomed to losing star players. He wanted to encourage Nicky's promotion to the Victorian league, but he was also keen for the Saints to pay some of what young Nicky owed South Freo. We reached an agreement in theory, which also involved transfer fees, but our plan could only be put into practice if Nicky was interested in coming to play for St Kilda. I'd have approached Nicky himself first but it was summer and he was back home with his parents in Pingelly, 158 kilometres from Perth, plus this was the first time I'd ever recruited anyone in my life, so I was winging it.

A friend of a friend was able to lend me a vehicle and I hit the road. The journey took me four or five hours in the sweltering 40-degree heat. This was before mobile phones or GPS or, in the vehicle I was driving, air-conditioning. I'd been brought up in the one of the coldest places on earth—Ballarat—so I was in all sorts of disarray by the time I reached my destination.

As I pulled up at Nicky's family's house, I saw there were no doors, no glass in the windows and the roof was falling off. An Indigenous fella without a shirt on was asleep on the doorstep in his undies, with a drowsy dog licking his foot. I gently woke the fella up and, while neither of us spoke each other's language, the name Winmar hit the spot. It became clear I was at the wrong place. There were no street names as such so the fella proceeded to show me where the Winmars lived by drawing me a map with a stick in the red dirt.

It wasn't long before I got out of the car at the actual Winmar home, which was in better shape than I'd expected and it was apparent the family had benefited from Nicky's WAFL contract. It was also the only house for some distance, but once I'd shut the car door behind me, people appeared from everywhere and were pointing me out to one other and speaking excitedly in their own dialect. I felt terrible internally but externally I had to give the impression that the move to St Kilda would be in everyone's best interests.

Fortunately Nicky made it immediately known it was in *his* best interests, because he'd been dreaming of playing VFL since he was a kid watching Keith Greig on ABC TV's *The Winners*. What followed was an interesting two or three hours because while Mum and Dad wanted their boy to follow his dreams, the reality of him being about to travel to the opposite side of the country was hitting home. Emotions were running high but Nicky's father in particular was adamant that this kind of footy career progression was what he'd dreamed of for Nicky since he was born. Once the tears subsided, Nicky's family requested an agreement that they'd be funded by the club to come visit their first-born boy—who they loved dearly—on a semi-regular basis. This was a fair and expected scenario upon which we quickly reached an agreement beneficial to all parties.

I asked Nicky when he thought he'd be ready to come to Victoria and I was surprised when he said, 'Are you heading to the airport now?' I told him that was correct and he said, 'Gimme a minute and I'll come with you.' It was a Saturday and on the long drive back to Perth, Nicky requested one last night there with his South Freo team-mates, so I stayed overnight while he partied, and we flew to Melbourne the next morning.

And that's how Nicky ended up at the Saints.

•

I recall a lot of what Graeme says but I also have it in my mind that a St Kilda footy club associate by the name of John King, who was a huge, 6-foot-4-inch, heavy-set Aboriginal fella with a black beard and moustache, *also* brought me to Melbourne on a flight from Perth. So what I reckon happened was that a week after landing in Melbourne with Graeme Gellie I became horribly homesick and, like I'd often done while at South Freo, I went home to Pingelly.

During that first week I remember calling Dad up and when he asked where I was (he thought I was still farewelling my South Freo team-mates), I told him I was in Melbourne and he didn't believe me. The Saints had seen me firsthand at training by that time, they'd heard the West Coast Eagles were having second thoughts about leaving me out of their 30-man squad, and it hadn't been long since Kevin Sheedy met with me, so it seemed they were worried when I went home that I might not come back. Or I would become an Essendon or West Coast player.

I'd not signed anything official at that stage and I was effectively still open to join any club I wanted. To my mind I was already a St Kilda player and I'd simply returned to Western Australia because I was keen to enjoy a few of my mum's home-cooked meals. But big John King was sent on a mission to get my arse on a return flight, quick smart. John and the Saints hatched a plan to sneak me out under the cover of a false name because they were paranoid that if word got out I was flying to St Kilda's home ground at Moorabbin, Kevin Sheedy might reconsider and make me an offer I couldn't refuse. John King told the lady at the check-in desk that my name was also John King, and so the two John Kings soon boarded a one-way flight to Melbourne.

Whatever the actual chain of events, one thing's for sure, I insisted my chocolate brown HX Kingswood had to be transported to Victoria. If the Saints were going to make me fly to Melbourne rather than drive across the Nullarbor, then they were responsible for making sure my wheels followed.

I'd previously been proud of my four-door Cortina, but once I could afford a HX Kingswood, I kicked that Cortina to the kerb. I can't recall the details now, maybe because I've locked the pain away, but my HX Kingswood was missing a few parts by the time it arrived at Moorabbin. I think it had travelled partly by train and partly by plane, and along the way some dirty bastards had cherry-picked pieces off it. And stolen my Jimmy Barnes cassingles out of the glove box too. The club was embarrassed about it, but I knew there wasn't much they could do. Promises were made about restoring my girl to her former glory but it never happened and I can honestly say, to this day, that I really DON'T CARE ANYMORE, okay?

I played 58 games for South Fremantle, kicking 98 goals between 1983 and 1986. With my time at South Freo behind me, it felt like four seasons in the WAFL had prepared me for what was ahead in Victoria.

# EIGHT

My first game for St Kilda was at VFL Park (renamed Waverley Park in 1990) in a pre-season Night Series Cup game against Essendon in 1987.

I was starstruck. I was out on the same ground as Bombers Billy Duckworth, Paul Vander Haar, Terry Daniher and Simon Madden. These guys were undisputed legends of the game. Premiership players. I felt like I was watching *The Winners* at home and somehow I'd jumped through the TV screen. Vander Haar was a courageous and spectacular double-premiership player, who former champion Collingwood player turned commentator Lou Richards had dubbed 'The Flying Dutchman', due to his high-marking prowess. When Tim Watson lined up alongside me I couldn't believe how huge he was, and when the game began, I couldn't believe how hard he was running. The man was like a locomotive. Then, at quarter time, out walked *the* Kevin Sheedy, whom I'd met before in a café, but here he was in action. It was hard to believe I was a part of it all.

My transition from Pingelly to Perth had been a culture shock, but my move from Perth to Melbourne (from 1 million people to 3 million people) made me feel like a grain of sand in the Sahara Desert. And the only black grain of sand. Compared to Perth there simply weren't any black people to be seen, no matter where I looked. Certainly no Aboriginals.

I would later learn that in suburbs such as Fitzroy I'd be more likely to find my people, but they were still few and far between. In the affluent bayside-ish areas of Moorabbin, and especially 25 Charman Road in Beaumaris, where the Saints arranged for me to share a house with team-mates Jamie Lamb (47 games for St Kilda and Geelong between 1986 and 1993) and Ben Ingleton (25 games for the Saints between 1985 and 1989), you were more likely to spot a Tasmanian Tiger than anybody Indigenous. The pace of Melbourne was impossible to keep up with too. Everybody was in a hurry, whereas I was from WA, an abbreviation we used to say stood for 'Wait Awhile'. In Melbourne nobody was waiting for nuthin. Except to get served by the bar staff in Transformers, a huge nightclub around the corner from our share house. You'd have to dance to stand a chance with the girls but it was worth it if you were hoping to wang chung tonight.

For a little while I was employed as a groundsman, maintaining the oval's vast grass surface alongside fellow new kid John Peter-Budge and our never-say-die State of Origin representative wingman Geoff 'Joffa' Cunningham. The main problem with that job was that I would rarely turn up and bother to actually do it.

I navigated pre-season training and instantly felt at home in the rooms after each session. The briny, tangy stink of men sweating in large numbers, working together towards a common goal, was a comfort zone I knew well. I was learning how to exist in the big city.

Then came my first real game in the big time. On the Thursday night, after training before Round 1 of the official 1987 VFL season, Darrel 'Doc' Baldock read the team off the whiteboard and I heard my name. I heard it again on the radio as I drove home.

Mum and Dad were flown in by the club, the first time on a plane for both of them. Our family used to watch planes going over our reservation sometimes and Dad would openly wonder what the experience might be like. 'Nerve-racking', was his assessment upon landing. Dad smoked a whole pack of durries straight after getting off the flight at Tullamarine, and immediately started making inquiries about whether he could drive back instead. Years after Dad's death, the aroma of a certain type of tobacco can make me momentarily wonder if my old man is somehow standing nearby.

Our Round 1 game was St Kilda versus Geelong at Moorabbin, my new home. I was 21 years old.

As we ran onto the ground the smell of sausages and onions cooking on a barbecue, brought along each week by a fan standing in the outer, was distracting. I hadn't realised I was hungry but those sizzling snags had my stomach grumbling, as they would do at every home game from then on.

A lot of the suburban grounds back then were mainly standing-room affairs. As was the case in the WAFL, VFL footy fans usually barracked for the team from the suburb they lived in. Carlton fans lived in Carlton, Hawthorn fans lived in Hawthorn and Richmond fans lived in Richmond. My team-mate Dean Rice also made his VFL debut that day, with Dwayne Russell and Mark Bairstow playing their first games for the Cats. It was weird competing against Mark Bairstow because we'd been team-mates at South Fremantle for the previous two years.

The Saints fans were a breed I'd never known before. You could sense the anxiety that a new season brought. Years of failure weighed heavily upon them.

Their hero went by the name of Trevor Barker, who justifiably wore the number one on his back. Barker was classy, courageous and could somehow sneak the entire team into the Melbourne Cup VIP tent with just one guest pass. His team-mates and Saints supporters adored him. He was like a beacon of light in stormy seas. Despite the club being on the brink of bankruptcy throughout the majority of his career, and despite holding the unfortunate league record of playing the most games without a final (230), Trevor refused countless more lucrative offers to join other teams, and famously donated a car he'd won for taking the Mark of the Year back to the club to raffle off as a fundraiser to help ensure his team-mates got paid what they were owed. Trevor was brilliant with the thousands of adoring kids who wore his number one on their back, patiently signing every autograph after every game, no matter how long it took him. You could see that women wanted to be with him and men wanted to be like him, including me, who'd seen Trevor taking all those amazing high marks on *The Winners* and wanted to do the same myself. He held the club together and in return the fans kept the faith.

Saints fans always saw the glass as half full and when they got behind us, especially at our home ground in Moorabbin, we felt like we could walk on water (which sometimes we had to, but I'll explain that later).

When the final siren sounded at the end of my first game, we'd lost by just one point but if not for the crowd we'd have lost by 30. I ended that game with the reasonable output of 13 kicks, four handballs and a goal.

On match days, if a chain of progressive handballs among St Kilda players gathered momentum, so did the crowd. Their affirmation was like a wave we could surf upon. You wanted to please them, you wanted to reward their undying belief in you, you wanted their approval, and if you got a shot of that, it was addictive. They were like Rocky Balboa's trainer, Mickey, riding the punches with you from the corner of the ring as the oppressive scent of beer burps and mass-produced hotdogs, made from a putrid pink meaty paste, polluted the air like a fog.

But before I'd even played a game for St Kilda, I met a very attractive young woman named Kelly. Within a couple of months we were living together in Keysborough. Our first child was soon on the way and I reacted like any mature 21-year-old who had just moved across the entire country from the bush to the big smoke would react when learning he was going to be a father. I bolted. Then I came back. And bolted again. Repeat. It's possible we were both as scared and excited as each other, but life was never boring, that's for sure.

In Round 11, I took the greatest mark of my entire life against Essendon, but it was in the shadows of the grandstand on an otherwise sunny day and the sole television camera had failed to adjust its lens quick enough to capture the moment satisfactorily (well, to my satisfaction anyway!). That mark can only be viewed in the dark, from just one angle. The roar of the crowd as I continued to rise, was, as Bette Midler would sing a year later, the wind beneath my wings.

In Round 19, we played Footscray at Moorabbin and the game was later described by VFL legend Kevin Bartlett as 'one of the greatest games I've seen in many, many years'. The Saints were a chance to win five games in a row for the first time since 1972, and for the first time since the 1960s a Saints game was sold-out in advance.

As I walked from the car park to the players' entrance, I saw several groups of fans (men, women and children) climbing over and crawling under the fences to get in. I realised we were creating something special.

The other memorable moment that day was seeing Footscray's Michael 'Magic' McLean walking into the ground to play against us. A hero to us Aboriginal wannabes, Michael was my age but had made his VFL debut four years earlier and had already become known for his anti-racism advocacy.

The Saints had been wooden spooners six times in ten years. If an AFL team was that bad for that long today, they would cease to exist. So while the idea of a premiership, or even playing finals, was beyond the most fanciful imagination of most Saints fans, it seemed almost certain we wouldn't win the wooden spoon that year, which was cause for celebration in itself. The other drawcard that day was that Tony 'Plugger' Lockett needed seven goals to become just the second St Kilda player ever to kick 100 in a season, since Bill Mohr back in 1936.

I truly didn't know who Tony Lockett was when I'd rocked up to pre-season training that summer and this young monolith approached me with his hand out to shake. 'G'day, mate, I'm Tony Lockett.' Now I remember that moment as one of my life's highlights.

The week of that Round 19 game, our coach, Darrel Baldock, had suffered a minor stroke and still hadn't left hospital. His former premiership team-mate Allan Davis stepped in for what would be the first of four games as fill-in coach. We planned to wear black armbands for a beautiful young boy named Matt Watts, a Saints fan born with spina bifida. Matt had been a regular around the club and was known as our 'Number One Brave Supporter', but sadly he had passed away. All in all it was set to be a big day with no shortage of motivation.

Both teams were neck and neck all day, with myself on the wing and our tough as teak centreman Greg Burns peppering our forwards with opportunities. Plugger kicked his seventh goal for the game (and hundredth for the season) in the last quarter, leading to Saints fans flooding onto the ground, before

Plugger managed one more that was also the match-winning goal, nudging us three points in front at the final siren. What *couldn't* the man do? For the first time all season I felt like we were a team that was going places, and fast.

Tony won the Coleman Medal for leading goal-kicker that year, the fourth St Kilda player to win it. He also became the seventh St Kilda player to win the Brownlow Medal. Plugger remains the only person in league history to win both the Brownlow and the Coleman in the same season. He also won St Kilda's best and fairest award, now called the Trevor Barker Award, *and* the Leigh Matthews Trophy (the Players' Association Most Valuable Player), all in that same year.

Plugger was good at partying hard too. When he won the Brownlow Medal, he had tied the award with Hawthorn's sensational South Australian recruit, Johnny Platten, so they got a medal each. The Rat, as Platten was known, had a head of long tight curly hair and he loved a beer with anyone, anywhere . . . except on this night. Platten had to head home early because his team was playing Carlton in the grand final on the Saturday. Plugger told him, 'Don't worry, mate, I'll get pissed for you too.' Being a man of his word, that's what the big fella proceeded to do. I know, because I was at the same table as the great man, alongside two of his other Ballarat-born buddies in Danny Frawley and Greg Burns. We'd all been told to rent tuxedos and I doubt we ever got our bond back because those monkey suits were as wrecked as we were.

For success-starved Saints fans, a Brownlow was worth getting excited about, and hundreds of them swarmed towards

Moorabbin Oval, straight after the televised medal count. There were so many St Kilda fans spontaneously crowding into the car park that word got out and the club decided they'd better open the bar. By the time we arrived, already buzzing from the free Brownlow booze, each of us having lost items of clothing along the way, the Saints' social rooms were jam-packed. When we walked in behind Plugger the atmosphere absolutely erupted. I'll never forget the sign behind the bar: 'There are no strangers here, only friends you haven't met yet'. And it was true, we had people we'd never met before sitting on our shoulders, we were giving piggybacks to blokes we didn't know, women were trying to pash-on with us without even saying hello, our heads were leaning back on the bar as beer got poured down our throats, Plugger was signing faces with permanent markers, and Cold Chisel songs were being belted out by happy idiots with their arms draped around each other. We danced and hollered and sang the club theme song until dawn.

But then came the morning after. I've never known a premiership hangover but if it's worse than the Brownlow version then maybe I'm lucky to have never played in a flag-winning team. Whoever kept buying me Frangelico that night has a lot to answer for (to this day I can't even look at a hazelnut). Sure, our behaviour doesn't say much for our professionalism, but forgive us for winning *something* for once.

My first season was over and I'd played 20 games (I'd missed Rounds 13 and 14 with a leg injury), kicked 37 goals and finished second in the Saints' best and fairest behind Plugger. I'd helped the Saints climb two rungs up the ladder (from last, in 12th position, to 10th) or even four rungs up, considering two new teams had entered the competition that year to make it a 14-team competition.

I had also polled ten votes in the Brownlow Medal, including two games where I was awarded the three votes for best on ground. We finished three games out of the finals, having lost three games by less than a goal.

The Saints had finished last in 1983, 1984, 1985 and 1986 and I am certain the immediate improvement came purely from my addition to the team. I'm equally certain that the fact we finished last on the ladder again the next season had nothing to do with me at all!

On 3 November 1987, Kelly and I welcomed our first baby into the world. A beautiful boy who we named Tynan. I held him in my arms as he took one look at me and burst into tears. As I soothed him I could swear he smiled. Either way, I thought, 'This is a dream come true.' Kelly was a natural mum from that moment on, and watching her bond with handsome little Tynan was lovely.

Back at the Saints we were all set to climb the ladder further but 1988 came and went and I'd rather not remember much of it.

We beat Geelong at Kardinia Park in Round 8 after I kicked the winning goal via a hard-fought handball from Plugger.

Due to Plugger being injured or suspended for the majority of the season, I became the club's leading goal-kicker with 43 goals and I came runner-up in the best and fairest again, this time to my captain Danny Frawley.

But it's a team game and we slid four spots down the ladder after winning just four games all year. We came last, 'winning' ourselves another bloody wooden spoon.

•

No matter how swiftly I'd adapted to the VFL, the weekly phone calls I shared with Dad between matches were often brutal, particularly after I'd played an ordinary game. Mum would answer my call and say, 'Dad doesn't want to come to the phone. He doesn't want to talk to you. He says you know why, you let him down by playing poorly.'

You might think my dad was being unnecessarily cruel, but back then we didn't know any different and tough love was how men communicated, if at all, both personally and professionally. All I knew was that Dad's opinion was more valuable to me than anybody else's, and he made sure to praise me when I played well so it wasn't as if he was never happy. If Dad was happy I was elated. Mum's thoughts on Dad's behaviour were never clear to me, possibly because she was too busy bawling her eyes out during each game, anticipating my certain death at any given moment.

Dad would listen on the radio when the game wasn't on TV, which was often because the Saints weren't any good at the time. This was before Foxtel or Kayo, where every game is televised. After giving me the silent treatment for days following a poor performance, Dad would eventually call and give me a mouthful before the next game. It might sound mean on his part, but wanting to please him is what drove me to maintain a high standard of play. While I genuinely respected every senior coach I had, none knew my game more than my dad. He didn't mind if I broke even with someone, but he hated me being beaten, even if my opponent was a highly rated player, or if I was tagged heavily by somebody whose only goal was to stop me from getting the ball rather than seeking the ball themselves.

•

We kickstarted the 1989 season with a six-goal win over the Brisbane Bears (before they merged with Fitzroy in 1996 and became the Brisbane Lions) at Moorabbin. Dad actually answered the phone when I called after that game, rather than waiting for Mum and me to chat first, so I knew he was happy with my game.

If I was ever to recommend watching a game (or part of a game) I played, I would tell you to watch St Kilda versus Carlton Round 2, 1989. With less than two minutes left in the game, Carlton were two points in front after the scores were level at three-quarter time. A boundary line throw-in results in my team-mate Jamie Lamb handballing out of defence to the wily veteran Ken Sheldon, who boots it towards the wing. Saints teenager 'Jack' Daniels gathers and handballs *long* to Winmar (that's me), who delivers a pass to the leading champion full-forward Tony Lockett, whose direct opponent, the official AFL Fullback of the Century, Stephen Silvagni, seemingly does everything right. Silvagni is in front, Lockett is behind, there is no way Silvagni can be beaten for that ball, but he is. Sure, my kick has to be perfect, and this is the one time I'll ever admit such a thing, but the kick *is* perfect.

Lockett has nine goals and is now lining up for his tenth, with 43 seconds to go. He kicks it and the Saints win their second of the season's opening two games.

These are the moments we live for, we train for, we sweat for, we bleed for. They are rare but they are unforgettable. Players spend so much time hating themselves for mistakes they made during games, after games, and often for the rest of their lives, so we also need to remind ourselves of the things we succeeded at.

By Round 16 on 22 July 1989, I was officially a married man. Kelly and I had our wedding the week before and, as the Saints were due to play the Brisbane Bears at their home ground in Carrara, the club sent us to Queensland a week early so we could enjoy a mid-season honeymoon away from the Melbourne winter. Plugger's uncle put us up at the Mardi Gras Resort in Broadbeach on the Gold Coast. We had to behave ourselves because Kelly was seven months pregnant with our second child and I had an upcoming game to play, but it was an enjoyable break nonetheless.

The Saints had lost our last five and the Bears had lost their last six so it wasn't expected to be a sparkling example of VFL footy, and yet it was a close one that saw the Bears get up by four points in the end.

What a shame it is when the second game of a season—the Lockett versus Silvagni show at Moorabbin—turns out to be that whole season's highlight, but that was the sad fact that year after we finished 12th.

We were treading water and as I watched that year's all-time great grand final between Hawthorn and Geelong, with its heroic battles all over the ground, I struggled to see how we could ever become a good enough team to compete in a grand final during my lifetime, let alone during my career.

We had six former Carlton players on our list by the time I arrived—several of whom had played in premierships but had been traded by Carlton because they'd lost their pace a little. One view was that we were a team full of recycled players past their prime, but another view was that our younger players (and the club as a whole) would benefit from the experience and professionalism of footballers who knew what it took to achieve the ultimate success. My view was that most of these guys really did set high standards, displaying the focus and will to win, both on and off the field, which the rest of us could learn from. However, whatever assets, real or imagined, these Carlton players did bring to the Saints, it didn't show on the scoreboard.

Another thing that didn't seem right was that the playing surface at Moorabbin was almost always an atrociously muddy bog-heap, even if there hadn't been any rain for weeks. This was because various high-up members of the club's administration believed that if they secretly saturated the ground the night before a home game (making the football heavy and the grass super slippery), it would bring the skills of our inevitably more talented opponents down to our level. Those same administrators apparently never stopped to consider that our team's already lesser skills might also be reduced even further. Luckily for me, I'd practised for hundreds of hours as a kid on those Pingelly lawns we'd soaked with hoses so we could replicate the Victorian conditions we'd seen on *The Winners*. The wet mud's smell reminded me of fertiliser, and in turn, sheep shit, which reminded me I was lucky to be chasing a Sherrin instead of still shearing.

I won the St Kilda best and fairest that season, which was scant consolation, but after finishing second in my first two years, winning the award at least showed I was personally improving. Rounds 20 and 21 (with Plugger out injured) saw me asked to play full-forward, where I kicked eight and nine goals, respectively.

I was also named in the VFL Team of the Year (what would later be called All-Australian). It was only a team on paper but I often wondered about the heights I (or any player) would have been able to achieve if the team was real and I was surrounded by these Rolls-Royces on every line.

| | | | |
|---|---|---|---|
| B: | A. Johnson, | C. Langford, | G. Pert. |
| HB: | B. Lovett, | G. Lyon, | G. McKenna. |
| C: | D. Pritchard, | P. Couch, | G. Brown. |
| HF: | N. Winmar, | S. Kernahan, | G. Ablett Sr. |
| F: | B. Stoneham, | J. Dunstall, | A. Bews. |
| Foll: | S. Madden, | M. Bairstow. | |
| Rover: | J. Platten. | | |
| Inter: | T. Daniher, | T. Watson, | M. Bayes, G. Williams. |

Somehow I'd gone from making my debut in the Pingelly seniors at the age of 15 to being named as one of the best 22 VFL players at the age of 24. It was a rapid rise beyond my wildest dreams, which made me feel more numb than anything else, because I didn't have the capacity to comprehend its scale.

After St Kilda's disappointing season, my year quickly took a turn for the better when Kelly gave birth to our daughter, who we named Shakira. She was the sweetest sight I'd ever seen since Tynan, when he was born. Shakira just gazed at me without blinking, as if we'd known each other forever. She stuck her gorgeous little bottom lip out, and seemed to stare into my soul. As I cuddled Shakira I'd rock her in my arms, as I'd done with my infant son, quietly singing 'The Wonder of You', as she drifted off to sleep.

# NINE

Around this time, a young footballer who would quickly develop into an all-time great was a regular speaker at Baptist church events around the country.

He approached me and asked if I'd consider religion as a way to structure my life outside of football. He asked if I'd ever seen or heard from God. I didn't think so but his question did make me wonder. In October 1989, I was due to attend a St Kilda end-of-season trip with my team-mates to Hawaii. But I had flashbacks to the Hong Kong trip with South Fremantle and decided at the last minute to go back to Pingelly instead.

There were issues at home, it was the middle of a pilot's strike, so I booked a train ticket to Western Australia. After I'd paid I asked how long the journey was and they told me it was three days. 'That's not long,' I thought, but how wrong I was. The minutes turned into hours turned into weeks turned into months. I lost track of what time it was, what day it was, as I drank all the way across the Nullarbor. There was nothing else to do. In 1989 the Australian cricket team's iconic Tasmanian batsman, David Boon, had sunk 52 cans on a flight to England. Before that, in 1986, Australian swimmer Neil Brooks had downed 46 cans on the flight home from the Edinburgh Commonwealth Games (where he'd won silver and gold medals). As a teenager with grand plans, I'd been a *tad* more disciplined than most of my fellow ratbag mates back in the day, but now it seemed I was making up for missed opportunities. If it was good enough for Aussie cricketers and swimming stars then it was good enough for me.

I kept up the pace once I arrived in Pingelly and had no shortage of old mates keen to join in. Then one night, after a billion beers, I looked at the sky as the sun was going down and I saw that the rising moon was a bright, blood red colour. It was gigantic and glowing and seemed close enough to reach out and touch. I was already in full self-loathing mode due to my complete absence of self-discipline, and I may have been hallucinating due to consuming copious amounts of booze across several hazy days, but I pointed towards the awesome crimson orb and asked my relatives, 'What the fuck is that?'

'It's a sign from God,' somebody said, without irony, and I burst into tears.

It was not long after that I considered converting to Christianity. I didn't, but I thought about it.

•

In 1990, it was the start of a new decade, a new league (the Victorian Football League was renamed the Australian Football League, in acknowledgement of the interstate teams joining the competition) and a new coach for the Saints. Our previous coach, the iconic Darrel 'Doc' Baldock, captain of the club's only premiership team back in 1966, had never seemed totally right after the second stroke he'd suffered towards the end of the 1989 season. When my team-mate and crafty defender Ken Sheldon retired at the end of that same season, he applied for the coaching role and got it.

Ken Sheldon was (and still is) an extremely calm, clever, friendly, decent and decisive man. He had been a truly brilliant rover for Carlton, and had kicked what became the winning goal in the 1979 Grand Final, before going on to be a triple premiership player for the Blues. As a Saints team-mate he was often the player to intercept the footy in our backline, before passing it to me in the midfield, whereupon I would ensure it landed in Tony Lockett's hands up forward, so Ken and I had enjoyed a healthy on- and off-field relationship. Ken Sheldon's presentation to the board when applying for the job of senior coach heavily emphasised his preferred assistant, Peter Hudson, as an extremely important part of the new regime. Among the approximately 13,000 men to have played VFL/AFL football, Peter Hudson still holds the record for most goals kicked per game, and he also equalled the record of 150 goals in a season (which he shares with South Melbourne's Bob Pratt). 'Huddo' averaged 5.64 goals a game over 129 games for Hawthorn, and like Sheldon, he was a premiership player too. These guys knew what to do. The board liked what they were told and appointed Sheldon, who was the last VFL player to switch straight from playing to coaching. Between them, Sheldon and Hudson became a dynamic duo who took us three rungs up the ladder to ninth in their first year together (1990).

One of the highlights of that year was beating Hawthorn for the first time in 20 attempts. Not since 1979 had the Saints won against the Hawks. During those same 11 years Hawthorn had played in seven grand finals, winning four premierships, while we had 'won' five wooden spoons, without playing a final of any kind.

Hawthorn had won the epic 1989 Grand Final against Geelong, so they were reigning premiers when they came to Moorabbin in Round 6 of the 1990 season. We'd won three of our first five games under Ken Sheldon, and had lost by just one point to Collingwood at the MCG the week before.

Hawthorn had won four of their first five games.

I knew I was in for a torrid afternoon when the consummate professional, Hawks captain Michael Tuck, lined up on me. The man was not only a superb footballer but his body was made up of hard, sharp, pointy angles. It was like playing against one of those triangular mathematical protractors. By the final siren we'd managed to break the drought. Our team won by three points in a thriller and our success-starved fans streamed onto the field, jumping for joy and hugging us all in tears while we hugged them right back.

I'd also experienced the personal satisfaction of playing well that day and, most memorably, jumping on Michael Tuck's back to take a massive high mark (and I had the puncture wounds from his pointiness to prove it).

•

Hawthorn champion Dermott Brereton owes me ten weeks' wages. To his credit, he's since publicly admitted to, and apologised for, racially vilifying me when Hawthorn and St Kilda met again that year in Round 19. I got suspended for ten games for retaliating and Dermott didn't miss a game at all, because racial abuse wasn't an offence in AFL footy in 1990.

It was an offence to me, obviously, which is why I kicked him in the balls after one particular remark, and I tried to gouge his eye out after another. I got reported for each offence and was suspended five weeks for each. It could have been worse though because I also delivered a straight left fist into his face at one point, which luckily for me the umpire didn't see. I'm talking like a tough guy here, but to be fair my team-mate Russell Jeffrey did have Dermott in a headlock at the time.

Dermott Brereton was a ruthless, talented, forceful, fearless player with a rarely matched will to win. I knew if I was to get into a fight with the man I'd better make it matter, but he left me with no choice and I left him thinking twice about upsetting me like that again.

In his newspaper column in *The Age*, on 18 August 1998, Dermott wrote how that afternoon in 1990 cost him some dignity. He mentioned how players knew they could put me and another player, West Coast's Chris Lewis, off our game by verbally abusing us, and that this abuse was racial.

Dermott wrote, 'I was never suspended for what I see now as a cowardly attack. If there was something I could change from my career, it would be the ugly comments I used to put those two players off their games, in what we thought back in those days was a part of the game ... I'm ashamed of what I did back then to provoke Nicky. But, with education, I have learnt from the error.'

Dermott's newspaper column made a lot of people sit up and take notice. I'm truly proud of Dermott for that. He has since apologised privately to me as well. Nowadays he's one of the most lovable larrikins I know. Always friendly and making jokes at his own expense. But first he sought to make reparations, for which I am grateful.

# TEN

Alongside Plugger, our other main forward at St Kilda during the early 1990s was the man with gigantic hands, Stewart Loewe. His vice-like grip saw him quickly average more than ten marks a game, most of them contested—amazing statistics that are rarely heard of today. Loewe would courageously charge into dangerous positions, but although he was arguably the best mark of the footy in the AFL, he was also arguably the worst kick.

Peter Hudson taught Loewe to count out a certain number of steps to mark himself a run-up as he prepared to take a set shot for goal, similar to what a fast bowler does before he runs in for his first over of the day. Seeing Loewe scratch out a line in the grass with his boot studs before lining up for goal was funny at first, but the laughs soon stopped as we saw how swiftly the technique succeeded. Loewe and Huddo continued to work hard and, after putting in countless extra hours at training, Loewe went from perhaps the most ordinary kick I'd seen to kicking 90 goals in a season. Maybe us team-mates shouldn't have been surprised, with the legendary Hudson lending a helping hand, but it was still an astonishing improvement.

The year 1991 saw three moments that had a major impact on my life. The first was our game against Collingwood in Round 4. They had beaten us by one point the season before and this time it was a draw. The scores were exactly level: 16.13.94 to 16.13.94.

The second moment was when I attended The Highwaymen concert at the Melbourne Tennis Centre (now Rod Laver Arena). The Highwaymen were a 'supergroup', comprising, in this instance, Johnny Cash, Willie Nelson, Kris Kristofferson and Waylon Jennings. Another supergroup, The Travelling Wilburys, featuring Bob Dylan, George Harrison, Roy Orbison, Tom Petty and Jeff Lynne had released an excellent album the year before, but The Highwaymen had been around since 1985. These guys were among the best solo singer–songwriters Mum and Dad had played endlessly at home and in the car through-out my childhood, so as I entered my fifth year since I'd moved to Melbourne and left my family behind, it was a great way to kind of emotionally catch up on old times.

Each of the four individual superstars took turns playing their own hits, with original Highwaymen songs in-between. If mobile phones had existed back then I would have Face-Timed Mum and Dad so they could have seen the concert and witnessed the fact that their boy had done well enough for himself to attend such a huge show in the first place. I'd have flown them in but they hadn't been keen on long flights since they'd come across for my first game in 1987.

That concert was one of the greatest nights of my life, which turned out to be an entrée for one of the best years of my life.

The third great moment of that year was that the Saints made the finals for the first time in 18 years.

We finished fourth on the ladder and, in any other year, that would have ensured we secured a 'double chance', meaning that even if we'd lost our first final we would have played another before being eliminated. Unfortunately, in 1991 they tried a final six system that meant if we lost our first final we were out. Yet, as Ken Sheldon told us at the first training session that week, it didn't matter as long as we won.

My great mate Tony Lockett had kicked 118 goals in the home and away games, including 34 goals in his first three games, having missed the first six games of the season with a back injury. I'd missed the first six games too, as part of my ten-week suspension from the incident with Dermott Brereton the previous year.

Unfortunately for Adelaide we'd both returned in the same game, which was Round 7 when we hosted the Crows at Moorabbin for the first time. Plugger and I were equally hungry to kickstart our seasons and we both helped our Saints to a 22-goal victory, 12 of those kicked by Plugger. It was a new club record for our greatest winning margin (24.18.162 to the Crows 4.7.31 adding up to a 131-point victory, eclipsing a 110-point win against Fitzroy in 1970).

Plugger followed up by kicking 10 goals against Brisbane in Round 8, and another 12 goals against Sydney in Round 9, before finishing with 13, 10 and 11 goals in the last three games before the finals.

Round 21 saw the debut of 22-year-old 'mature age' recruit Dean Greig, who we'd snapped up from Camberwell. More than 30 years later he still holds the record for most disposals on debut, officially listed in AFL records as 39 (although he swears the Saints' statisticians recorded 41). Dean went on to play 33 games, many of which were close ones against Collingwood in front of huge crowds, and he was excellent in most of them. A hard-as-nails midfielder, the man remains one of my great mates.

•

The build-up to that first Saints final for 18 years was phenomenal. The club's car park was packed full of news vans. Thousands of fans turned up to training every night, which created a consistent rush of adrenaline the likes of which I'd never experienced.

Myself and three team-mates—Lockett, Loewe and our exceptionally tough defender David Grant—were named All-Australians that year. Our captain Danny Frawley had also been in fantastic form, as had a couple of fast-rising, hard-running midfielders in Robert Harvey and Nathan Burke—both of whom would go on to be inducted into the AFL Hall of Fame. All of that combined to make us a feared AFL outfit that season. My Indigenous brother Gilbert McAdam's sparkling first season with the Saints added an X-factor that made us confident we were a big chance to win our final against Geelong at Waverley Park.

Geelong boasted a brilliant midfield of Mark Bairstow, Paul Couch, Andrew Bews and Garry Hocking, but it was the always intimidating Gary Ablett Sr's ability to also inflict injury that had its own impact because by quarter time he'd crunched both Nathan Burke and David Grant out of action.

This being the era of 20 players per team, we had no spare men from quarter time onwards.

We were ten points behind at quarter time, 19 points in front at half-time, but while Lockett kicked 9.5, Geelong's Billy Brownless kicked 8.3 in a four-quarter goal-for-goal showdown, ending with the Cats winning by seven points. AFL players are often accused of uttering clichés in after-match interviews but I was telling the truth when I said after the final siren that, given the choice, I'd have swapped what was personally a prominent performance for a win by the team (a fact that applied to every game I ever played). I finished the game wearing number 60, after my usual number 7 had been ripped off my back in a brutal tackle by Geelong's ruckman Stephen Hooper. Thirty years later, in September 2022, that torn number 7 was given back to me by a collector who found it in his garage as he was moving house. And 30 years later, I'd still swap it for a win that day.

Those nine goals from Plugger in that 1991 Elimination Final took him to 127 for the season. (At that season's average of seven goals a game, he might have finished with another 42 goals, for a total of 169, if he'd played every game). Shortly after the finals, Collingwood's president Allan McAllister invited our coach Ken Sheldon and our then president, Travis Payze, to a meeting at the East Boundary Hotel in Bentleigh. McAllister informed Payze and Sheldon that Collingwood wanted to buy Tony Lockett, and right then and there he offered . . . one million dollars.

Payze was perhaps keen to hear more because the Saints at that stage (and indeed at many stages) of their history were not flush with cash, but Sheldon knew that with Lockett gone, he would probably soon follow. Sure, it may have been a partly selfish motive, but he also knew that Lockett provided the club's long-suffering supporters with the most valuable commodity in footy: hope. Sheldon gave Plugger and me hope too. I hoped he would keep allowing me to miss training occasionally (usually due to being thirsty that day but I'd claim to be injured or unwell instead). Plugger hoped Sheldon would keep letting him take occasional weekdays off to race his greyhounds around the country. I don't mean to be painting a picture of Sheldon being a pushover (he wasn't), but some players, especially if they're among the competition's elite, can benefit from being given an extra-long leash. Geelong coach Malcolm Blight faced the same situation with Gary Ablett Sr at times.

I remember laughing out loud the day Plugger wanted to drive to Orange in New South Wales with one of his dogs for the second week in a row, and Sheldon said, 'Mate, I could be wrong but I'm not sure being sat in a car for 800 kilometres each way is the ideal preparation for an AFL player, especially when, during the 20-hour round trip, you'll be eating nothing but fucken dim sims.'

When I was named in the AFL All-Australian team for the first time, officially, in 1991, I couldn't shut Dad up on the phone that night. Nor did I want to.

# ELEVEN

A lot has been said about the St Kilda Football Club being full of party boys over the years, and it's true, but we weren't alone. The difference was we had our own nightclub at our club's headquarters.

Obviously that's a recipe for disaster, but the money spent on entrance fees and over the bar at the infamous 'Saints Disco' probably kept us financially afloat for longer.

The Saints Disco was based upstairs at Moorabbin. It was open every Friday night, and on Saturdays after home games. It was an expectation after those home games that we players would stick our heads in for a beer or two so the fans who'd hung around would get to rub shoulders with the stars. The major problem with that plan was that we lost way more games than we won, so everyone entered the venue unhappy, and *then* they got on the grog.

Us players were given a free dinner after home games but we were expected to eat it at tables in a barely separated side section of the nightclub, often with our wives and kids in tow. Plenty of punch-ups took place in such a confused and erratic environment. Plugger once decked the club's general manager after a well-oiled argument and I once decked a bloke who thought it would be funny to grab my toddler's teddy bear and chuck it out onto the dancefloor.

A lot of our opponents stayed around after the games too, and there were many occasions when I enjoyed bonding with blokes I'd been battling against only hours earlier. When I'd had my share of Southern Comfort and cokes by the time 'Underneath the Radar' came on, John Travolta would've been envious of my fancy dancefloor feet.

The Richmond Football Club also had its own nightclub at their Punt Road HQ but most clubs tended to hang out at specific city-based nightclubs, such as, in Collingwood's case, The Tunnel. The 1980 Richmond premiership team, the 1990 Collingwood premiership team and the Carlton premiership teams of the 1980s were all known for loving a drink too, but they all avoided criticism because they got the job done, whereas we did not. I can see the merit in the differentiation, but it's not like every other team except the Saints comprised tee-totalling choirboys tucked into bed each night by 8 pm. In fact, Trevor Barker retired in 1989 and at his testimonial night (before the big money entered the game, club legends would have a farewell function arranged for them upon their retirement, with all proceeds going to the departing star), half the crowd (all of whom were as drunk as it's possible to be) were stars from opposition sides, including teams at the top of the ladder.

One of those players was Collingwood's Darren Millane, and almost two years to the day after Barker's retirement night, Darren Millane lost his life at age 26 in a car accident after a huge night at The Tunnel. I loved Darren as a player and as a man. I can't claim we were best mates but he was a great guy. He often hung out at the Saints Disco (even if Collingwood had played elsewhere that afternoon), we respected each other's abilities, we were both hard at the ball, and we were both living wild lifestyles, even if I was attempting to present publicly as a stable family man, while somehow managing to maintain career-best form out on the field. I was All-Australian in the year of his death and he'd been All-Australian the year before, when his Magpies won the premiership. Darren's fate could probably have befallen a lot of us, from many clubs, on any other night, heading home worse for wear. I'd say a large percentage of top footballers in that era were adrenaline junkies who were out on the town at least three nights a week.

As a sporting industry we were shocked by Darren's demise but we had no right to be. If any settling down after Darren's death did occur, our league-wide conduct as blokes who worked hard and played harder came roaring back to peak party-time in the late 1990s when the North Melbourne Football Club won two premierships. They were as unbeatable off the field as they were on it. I suppose our attitude was like that classic Richard Clapton song 'The Best Years of Our Lives'.

Even though Darren Millane's life was tragically cut short, and his wasn't a lifestyle I'd recommend to anyone (having enjoyed and endured it myself), he didn't waste time, and they really were the best years of his life. And mine.

Every AFL player was saddened by Darren's loss but we had no choice but to get back to preparing for the coming season.

# TWELVE

Just as my year training at South Fremantle during the summer of 1986 had been soundtracked by the Warumpi Band's 'Blackfella/Whitefella' song, so was St Kilda's training throughout the summer of 1991–92 soundtracked by Yothu Yindi's smash-hit 'Treaty'.

That summer also saw the Saints recruit a member of a renowned Indigenous 'footy-legacy' family: Dale Kickett. Dale had played a season with Fitzroy before going back to Western Australia to play for the West Coast Eagles. He only managed two senior games but played for Claremont in the WAFL later that year, where he was awarded the Simpson Medal for best on ground in the grand final and won his second WAFL premiership medal. He played the 1992 season at the Saints, before returning to Claremont, where he yet again won the Simpson Medal in a premiership team.

What a season he had with us though. Twenty-one games for 20 goals was a classy contribution, and it was enjoyable for me as I got to play alongside yet another blackfella. That meant there were three of us in the Saints line-up, the other being my brother-in-arms, the incredibly talented Gilbert McAdam.

Gilbert was one of eight children, three of whom played AFL football. His older brother Greg had played ten games for the Saints in 1985. In 1989, aged 22, Gilbert became the first Aboriginal to win the Magarey Medal, awarded to the best and fairest player in the SANFL (South Australian Football League). He had joined us from Central Districts in South Australia in 1991.

Gilbert McAdam, Russell Jeffrey, Jimmy Krakouer and I played in numerous games together, which may have been a St Kilda record, until Round 4 of 2022 when seven black-fellas lined up for the red, white and black against Hawthorn at Marvel Stadium.

Russell Jeffrey was a Darwin-born defender whose family were evacuated to Melbourne when he was eight, immediately after the wreckage caused by Cyclone Tracy in 1974. (I had family in Darwin, who had departed two days before the cyclone. We'd asked them, 'Did you have a sixth sense about it, from our ancestry's connection to the sun, the earth, the water and the wind?' They said, 'No, we heard the warnings on the radio.') Russell played 14 games for us in 1988, leaving to become a bush premiership coach in Ned Kelly country at Jerilderie in 1989, before returning to play 20 games for the Saints in 1990, as well as representing Victoria in State of Origin games.

Another Aboriginal team-mate I played with was Bob Jones, who debuted at the mature age of 26, played 20 games in his first season for the Saints as a ruckman who rested in defence, only to badly do his knee in the first round of the 1989 season, after which he never played again. His contribution to the game continued through his son Liam Jones, who has played for the Western Bulldogs and Carlton.

Another Saints ruckman by the name of Jones—Warren 'Wow' Jones—became an honorary blackfella in my mind when he told me during my first season that if anyone gave me any racist crap, I should let him know at once. Wow had played as the back-up ruckman to Mike Fitzpatrick in Carlton's 1982 premiership team. He was 6 foot 7 inches tall, 34 years old and his nickname originated from a rumoured pair of Ws tattooed on his arse. One on each cheek, so if he bent over, the word that became his nickname appeared before your eyes. During a game against North Melbourne in my first season, aged 21, I had reason to dob an opposition player in to my new man-mountain mate Wow, who promptly lifted the offender upside down by his ankles and told him he'd be dead if he bothered me again.

Last but not least, in 1998, St Kilda recruited Indigenous roving forward Gavin Mitchell from Fremantle and he kicked 22 goals from 23 games in his first season with us.

Gavin played at the highest level during five seasons, for 88 games. That's a lot of hours, weeks, months and years on the training track, in the weights room, watching videos of both your own previous game and that of your next opponent. It's a lot of team meetings, a lot of whiteboard studying and a long time eating entirely healthy food. When the average amount of games played by AFL players is just 30, the dedication and skills required to stay at the top for 100, 200, 300 or even 400 games is pretty much beyond comprehension.

I am proud of my 251-game career but there are 266 players who played more games than I did. Not forgetting that my dedication to training and team meetings, or even my willingness to regularly attend training and team meetings, left a lot to be desired.

Aboriginals from Western Australia, who had to acclimatise to the comparatively big city of Melbourne, homesick as hell every single day and night, 2770 kilometres from home, missing our families, landscapes and cultures something chronic—along with every other Indigenous player who's had to move to mainly white, urban areas (from, effectively, the outback) if we wanted to compete with the best—should all feel proud of ourselves, whether we played one career game, 88 like Gavin Mitchell, or 407 like the silky Shaun Burgoyne did for Port Adelaide and Hawthorn.

# THIRTEEN

In 1992 I was proud to play my 100th game against West Coast Eagles at Subiaco Oval, the same ground where I played my first senior game for South Freo in the WAFL. Mum and Dad made the trip but Dad wouldn't speak to me afterwards because we lost by four goals, even though I had 18 touches and kicked two goals. Mum tried to explain but I couldn't make out much of what she said due to her crying with relief that I'd completed the game without losing my life to injury. I swear I could smell her roast lamb through the phone that night.

We started the season well, winning several games, and in Round 12 St Kilda defeated Collingwood by one point in front of just over 80,000 spectators at the Melbourne Cricket Ground on the Queen's Birthday holiday. It was the biggest crowd I'd ever played in front of and when I kicked what would be the second last goal of the game, to put us just five points behind with ten minutes to go, the sound of the crowd was exhilarating. Only slightly less so than the sound they made when my team-mate Craig Devonport kicked the last goal of the game a few minutes later to secure us the victory.

Craig's goal was also significant because earlier in the game Ken Sheldon had left the coaches' box up in the stand, reached over the fence and aggressively grabbed Craig by the scruff of his jumper to remind him of some basic match-play tactics that Craig seemed to have forgotten. Craig could have sulked, he could have justifiably held a grudge against Ken for his vigorous and potentially embarrassing public approach, but Craig took Ken's insights on board and when the opportunity arose to apply those tactics later in the game, it led to Craig winning the game off his own boot. Credit to Ken too, for gauging Craig's ability to absorb criticism, when it could have backfired on them both. It was a concise example of how tough it must be to coach a team of human beings. In the AFL there are 42 players on a club's list and for a coach to correctly guess how each one of them prefers to be motivated, depending on their fixed nature or their mood at any given time, is a level of witchcraft I can't begin to imagine. I can barely manage or understand my own mind, let alone the minds of 42 other people. Some would say it's just trial and error but the errors can see some individuals lose faith in you forever.

Not long after that, during Round 16 at the MCG, Essendon's Kieran Sporn received a sublime short pass from Derek Kickett and kicked long into the Bombers' forward line to his unmanned team-mate Todd Ridley. Sporn kicked it so high, my instincts and experience combined to calculate that if I sprinted at full pace I might have time to make Ridley earn the ball.

As I approached I understood I'd need to elevate if I was to even get a hand on the ball, so I leapt into the air and, somehow as I flew sideways and backwards simultaneously, my leg landed on Ridley's back, which gave me just enough purchase to defy gravity for long enough to reach the footy with my right hand. I pulled it into my chest and landed hard from a great height, flat onto my coccyx bone. I couldn't help being aware of the entire crowd (Essendon fans included) going berserk.

At season's end I was awarded a Mitsubishi Magna for Mark of the Year. I traded the Magna in for an HSV, but by the end of my career I reckon I should have had my own bloody car yard.

Round 20, 1 August 1992, was St Kilda's last ever game at Moorabbin after 27 years and 254 games. The Saints hadn't been able to win a single premiership at their previous home ground, the Junction Oval in St Kilda, but just one year after switching to Linton Street, Moorabbin, the 1966 Premiership was ours. It remains the Saints' first and only premiership so far.

That day we beat our opponents, Fitzroy, by 18 points in a scrappy game, yet what sticks in my memory and still gives me goosebumps to this day is the outpouring of emotion from Saints fans when the final siren sounded. Tens of thousands of fans poured onto the ground and cried en masse, hugging the players tight as we tried to get off the ground. The fans on the ground faced the fans in the grandstand and both groups sang the famous team theme song—'Oh When the Saints Go Marching In'—back and forth to each other for almost an hour, as sausages sizzled in the standing room one final time.

I'd been lucky enough to play my first senior game at Moorabbin in Round 1 of the 1987 season and that last Moorabbin game was my 117th. The club and its base had effectively been my home for the first five years of my life in Victoria. I'd become married, had kids and established myself as an AFL player while we were at Moorabbin so it wasn't just the fans who shed tears that day.

The AFL was keen on herding the majority of clubs from their original home grounds towards Waverley Park (formerly VFL Park) and the MCG. The club had no choice but to obey the AFL's demands that we relocate to Waverley Park, because the financial situation was more beneficial and as always we were broke. Later, in 2000, when Waverley Park was abandoned, the Saints were sent to a brand-new Docklands home venue, now called Marvel Stadium.

In our last game of the season, we were two points down at three-quarter time against Melbourne at the MCG in atrocious conditions. Each team had only scored four goals in torrential rain and gale-force winds.

Not only did we need to win but we needed to win by four goals to make the finals. At three-quarter time, Ken Sheldon told us all to clear the forward line and kick it to Lockett at every opportunity. 'We need four goals, Plugger,' Sheldon told the great man. 'That's as many goals off your own boot in this final quarter as the whole team has kicked in the first three quarters so far. What do you reckon?' Plugger nodded confidently as the wind and rain lashed his face in the huddle. 'Yeah, I'll kick four goals.'

Four goals from Plugger later, we'd won the game and were in the finals.

•

Everything I'd trained for, every drop of sweat and blood, every tear I'd shed, was in search of this moment. Well, *the* moment would be winning a premiership, but for now, winning our first ever final would do.

We led Collingwood by a solitary point at the first break, and nine points at half-time. Jamie Shanahan was nullifying Peter Daicos in the back half, while Robert Harvey was tearing Mick McGuane apart in the engine room.

My 23-year-old team-mate Mick Dwyer, who had earlier won the 1992 Gardiner Medal for the best player in the reserves competition, had a fantastic second half and finished with 27 disposals and two goals.

Eight of Plugger's nine disposals were shots for goal, five of which went through the middle. He was aided by Stewart Loewe, who starred at centre half-forward, while Harvey was best afield, amassing 34 possessions.

We'd beaten Collingwood in the elimination final. The footy world was our oyster. We just knew this was going to be our year.

But we were wrong. We lost the semifinal the following Saturday to Footscray by 29 points and then didn't win another final until the 1997 qualifying final against the Brisbane Lions, five long years later.

# FOURTEEN

'You should be hung from the nearest tree you fucken dogs.'

That's just one of the remarks shouted at Gilbert McAdam and me on that infamous day at Victoria Park, home ground of the Collingwood Football Club.

Before the game even started.

'We're going to kill your whole fucking family!' was another.

All we planned to do was stroll casually out onto the field during half-time of the reserves game, before the main game, to see how wet the ground was and how the ball bounced. As we strode up the players' race, the first section of crowd we encountered was the Collingwood Cheer Squad, most of whom unleashed a torrent of abuse worse than either of us had experienced in our lives—and believe me, we'd copped racist abuse before. Every blackfella has, but this stuff was chilling. People promising they'd rape my mum, the works.

On Saturday, 17 April 1993, Round 4, a capacity crowd of 28,350 had crammed into Victoria Park, Collingwood's home ground, expecting an epic encounter.

It was the Match of the Round. Collingwood was coming off a five-day break, having beaten Essendon by 30 points at the MCG on Easter Monday to sit second on the ladder and be one of only two unbeaten sides with Adelaide. The Saints were sixth on the ladder, having accounted for the Swans and North Melbourne, but our task was made more difficult by entering the match without Tony Lockett, who had kicked eight goals against the Swans at Waverley Park the week before but had been suspended for two games for striking Tony Malakellis.

Our All-Australian defender David Grant was out with a broken thumb and our number one ruckman Lazar Vidovic missed the game with a quad injury. During the match, Robert Harvey, who was starring with 14 disposals, tore a quad muscle, and Dean Greig strained his hamstring.

The last time we'd won at Victoria Park was in 1976, 17 years earlier. We stood little chance of winning.

And it was bloody hot that afternoon too, one of the hottest April days on record.

Gilbert McAdam had been racially abused by Collingwood players in three games between the teams before the 1993 encounter at Victoria Park. As had I, but I'd become used to it, kind of, by then. Gilbert has always refused to name names but in an interview with journalist Caroline Wilson in the *Sunday Age*, on the eve of the 1991 Finals series, Collingwood captain

Tony Shaw had this to say: 'I'd make a racist comment every week if I thought it would help win the game. If I think I can say something to upset someone, then I'll say it. I couldn't give a stuff about their race, religion or creed. If they react, you know you've got em.

'If they're going to get upset by taunts, then they shouldn't be playing. We're men, we're not kids. It's no different calling a bloke a black bastard than him calling me a white honky, and it only lasts as long as the game. And listen, any bloke in the history of footy who was a dead-set winner will tell you the same, they'll do anything they can to win.'

Tony Shaw changed his ways a long time ago and I no longer have a problem with him whatsoever. In fact, we get along in a very friendly fashion these days.

But when Gilbert and I walked onto the ground at half-time of the reserves game that day, the Collingwood Cheer Squad started on us. A stench of rum, hashish and hatred seeped from the Magpies fans' pores. The hideous stuff they were shouting was bad enough, but they were spitting on us too. And worse. Someone tipped liquid on me as I ran onto the ground. I thought it was water but then I sniffed my jumper. It was piss.

When we got to the centre of the ground, Gilbert grabbed me and said, 'Brother, we have got to do something today. We can't put up with this crap. We have got to make a statement. We will show this mob . . . we've got to make them quiet. Me and you have got to get best on ground out here. The only way we can stick it up them is to be better than everyone else and to win this game. You and I need to lead the way.'

111

All I could do was nod in agreement. We shook hands and ran the ugly gauntlet of Magpie fans spitting on us back into the rooms.

The build-up of the previous close games between the teams, the venue packed with mainly Collingwood fans, the unseasonal heat and the extra alcohol consumed because of that heat, all added up to an atmosphere of negative energy I've never experienced before or since. This crowd was baying for blood. Aboriginals were not welcome and they were letting us know it. We felt like shit, like they didn't consider us to be the same species as them.

On top of everything else, it obviously wasn't the ideal pre-game preparation. Gilbert and I kept our pact to ourselves, maybe because none of our team-mates had heard the comments and, being white, they wouldn't feel how it hurt.

The game began and, by God, did Gilbert and I live up to our word. I had previously played games where I was shithouse, uninterested, hung-over, beaten by a better opponent, but not this day. On this day I saw everything unfolding before anyone else, like the game was sticking to a script that only me and Gilbert had read in advance. Some of the sheer athletic and intellectual majesty Gilbert displayed with the ball in his hands that day was artistic genius. Gilbert had five goals before three-quarter time and was running rings around every Collingwood player on the ground. I wasn't far behind him and when the final siren sounded we'd won by 22 points, after kicking seven goals to three in the third quarter. Gilbert and I embraced each other in the centre of the ground. 'We did it brother! We showed em!' he shouted.

•

Gilbert received three Brownlow Medal votes for his 21 disposals and five goals, while I received two Brownlow votes for my 25 disposals and a final-quarter long-range goal on the run, which sealed the upset victory.

What we didn't know at game's end was that Gilbert's dad, Charlie, had left the ground before quarter time, saddened and sickened by the malicious abuse aimed at his son. Back in his hotel, Charlie McAdam listened in tears to the rest of the game he had travelled from Alice Springs to see. Tears of frustration and fury. 'How could this be, in a big city in 1993?' he thought. What had his son done to deserve such verbal violence, except play good footy? Is that not what a crowd wants to see?

As we walked from the ground, victorious at Victoria Park, the sound coming from the Collingwood supporters scared me, and I don't jump at shadows.

The twisted faces of hostile hatred, the spittle-flying fury, the threats I'll never forget, all aimed directly my way, combined into a scenario that still makes me shudder. I didn't know what to do. I didn't want them to see how I was genuinely afraid for my safety, worrying that I might not get out alive (truly, that thought ran through my mind). The words 'black c*nt' swarmed my way like locusts, from the mouths of thousands, and I thought I might throw up.

Then my dad's words came back to me. 'Don't take no shit from nobody,' he used to say, and so I lifted my St Kilda footy jumper with one hand, and pointed to my skin with the other hand.

'I'm black and I'm proud to be black,' I shouted—for the crowd, for myself and for my ancestors.

For the next ten seconds, I stood still, holding that pose in a moment of pure power. I hadn't planned the response but it felt like . . . love . . . which always wins over hate. It felt like I sent a message to my elders, and from my elders, past, present and emerging. It felt like the land I stood on owned me, and I, in turn, owned the land. The earth, myself and the sun were as one. Then the waves of appalling abuse came roaring back. The hatred, unlike the sound for that brief moment, had not gone away. I'd just managed to zone out for as long as it took to rescue my soul and my self-esteem.

# FIFTEEN

Down the players' race I ran to belt out the Saints' theme song, arm-in-arm with my team-mates, because this was a win for the ages, and I'd survived. Or I thought I'd survived.

When my wife Kelly and our kids came into the dressing rooms, the look on their faces was shock and disbelief. The language and the death threats they'd heard aimed my way all day had frozen them. Unlike Gilbert McAdam's dad, who'd managed to escape early on, Kelly had thought it was too big a risk to try to get the kids out of the ground. She worried what might happen if the Collingwood fans recognised that she was my wife. She wondered if the Aboriginal DNA of our kids was visible, and what that recognition might lead to.

I'd never publicly spoken a word against the Collingwood Football Club, I'd never been reported for striking one of their players, there was no logical basis for the loathing, except for the fact that I was black. That's not me being paranoid, that's not a chip on my shoulder, that's the sheer fact of the matter.

The Saints club officials surrounded my family and me as the police came to discuss ways of sneaking us out of the ground. By now I'd become fully frightened. Were these people going to lynch me? Try to harm my wife and children? What was my crime? I'd simply played a good, fair game of footy and, in exchange, a large number of haters were now waiting for me outside. If I'd reacted to the disgraceful stuff shouted at me all day by abusing the crowd back, by yelling angrily in *their* direction, by sticking my middle finger up at *them*, I guess that would have upset the crowd also.

I understood that my team had won but I personally couldn't win.

I thanked the police but assured them my family and I would be fine. I didn't believe that statement for a moment but I thought police involvement might escalate the situation. I asked some senior club officials how they thought I might get home and they strongly suggested I didn't go home at all that night.

A little while later they said they'd had an idea. Kelly, the kids and I were smuggled out a back door and into a waiting vehicle. I asked where we were being taken. 'To Molly Meldrum's house,' I was told.

Molly Meldrum had been Australia's most famous and popular music expert for decades, having come to prominence as the mumbling yet lovable host of the ABC's Sunday night TV staple, *Countdown*. When that show ran its race, Molly moved on to probably the second most iconic TV show in Australian history, *Hey Hey It's Saturday*, where he regularly secured the only Aussie interviews granted by the likes of Madonna, Elton John and Michael Jackson, whenever artists of that stature wanted to promote a new tour or album down here.

Molly is a massive long-term Saints fan who was at the MCG in 1966 when St Kilda won their only premiership, and as a worshipper of the team, he'd made himself known to generations of Saints players. He and I had always got along well and I felt I'd known him all my life, having welcomed him into my childhood corrugated iron shack each Sunday night on TV.

Who knows if me being black and Molly being gay forged an understanding of each other's 'outsider' status, but from the day we met we've felt like brothers. We've always been close and I've crashed at Molly's many times after his many outrageous parties.

This night after the Collingwood game, however, was no party. There was heavy drinking, but of a different kind. We may have won that day but we weren't celebrating. Once we'd got the kids off to sleep, Kelly, Molly and I sat around with a bottle of red, or four, and wondered what the immediate future looked like. This wasn't America's deep south in the 1950s, it was Melbourne, Australia, in 1993, and I was in hiding from lots of white people who hated me simply because my skin was black.

The next morning, before I could consider whether we'd possibly overreacted by not going home the previous night, the police arrived at Molly's with a couple of Saints board members, holding several letters that had been left at both my house and the footy club overnight. The contents of those letters, handwritten by people identifying themselves as Collingwood supporters, mentioning members of my family by name (including our children), were so repulsive that I still genuinely shudder whenever I think about them. I cannot, and will not, bring myself to recall the exact wording on those pages, but let's just say that those letters made the 'rape' remarks seem like Christmas cards. I continued to receive similar missives for months afterwards.

As I later told the exceptional Indigenous journalist Karla Grant, in those days nobody had mobile phones but people hated me so much they bothered to sit down and write it in a letter. Then hand deliver it. Why? I didn't say anything bad about anybody. I didn't *do* anything bad to them. My actions spoke louder than words. I said a positive thing about myself, in response to them saying negative things about me and my family. Am I supposed to just take that abuse? I mean, how are they more angry than I am in that situation?

The Saints board members also brought copies of that day's newspapers. My photo was on the front page of *The Age*, accompanied by a story by the excellent journalist Nick Place, which ended up making history.

But my heart was broken and my mind was a mess. I didn't want to participate in the world around me, let alone set foot on a footy field again. As I weighed up the question of 'What's next?', Collingwood's president Allan McAllister was questioned at a press conference about the behaviour of his team's supporters towards Gilbert McAdam and me. I was watching it live on television and if I expected him to be apologetic or at least display a smidgeon of concern or kindness, I could not have been more wrong. It was difficult to believe my eyes and ears back then, and it's still impossible to believe all these years later.

In front of dozens of cameras, microphones and journalists, McAllister said, 'As long as they [Aboriginal people] conduct themselves like white people off the field, everyone will admire and respect them.'

I wonder if he meant the white people who'd said such repulsive things about my mum, or the white people who'd written the letters containing terrifying threats towards my children, by name? Did he mean the white people who'd spat in my face as I left the field at Victoria Park? The white people who'd made Gilbert McAdam's dad leave the ground sobbing before quarter time? Were these the people he wanted us to behave like? Were these the benchmarks of humanity he was speaking about?

McAllister's press conference was supposedly intended to settle the situation down but only made matters worse.

And he wasn't finished yet. 'As long as they conduct themselves like human beings, they will be all right. That's the key.'

Like human beings?

This wasn't a defensive remark in the heat of the moment from a man being instinctively loyal towards his troops.

This wasn't a man who was drunk or under the influence of drugs.

This wasn't an uneducated or unemployed man, a man from a low socio-economic background who didn't know any better.

This was the President of the Collingwood Football Club. An organisation that has long self-described as the Manchester United of Australian sport, the most powerful club in the nation.

Allan McAllister was successful in business outside and inside of football, he had a platform and his opinions were influential. I don't wish to speak ill of the dead (he passed in 2019) and I hope he was a loving family man whose absence leaves a hole in the lives of many, but how did he not address the fact that Collingwood supporters needed to clean up their act in the aftermath of that week, following the worst day of my life? Of my family's lives? The worst day in the lives of Gilbert McAdam and his dad?

Was I supposed to take McAllister's advice and study up on how to behave like the mythically moral white people he was referring to? Would there be an exam to see if I successfully met the criteria? Who would mark my work? If I was eventually considered worthy of *human being* status, by whoever passed final judgement, how would I benefit? How, exactly, would I be 'all right', as he had promised?

Allan McAllister managed to stay at the helm of the Collingwood Football Club for another two years. How?

# SIXTEEN

People may say 'it was a different time' but it was 1993. Greater political, legal and cultural progress had arguably been achieved during 1991 to 1993 than in any other three-year period of our history as a modern nation. In fact, 1993 had been declared as the International Year for the World's Indigenous People.

In 1991, Yothu Yindi became the first Indigenous musical artists to win the APRA Song of the Year, with their smash hit 'Treaty'.

On 3 June 1992, after a ten-year battle, the famous Mabo legal judgment overturned the myth that at the time of colonisation, Australia was 'terra nullius', or 'uninhabited land belonging to no one'. The High Court of Australia decided that terra nullius should not have been applied to Australia and acknowledged that Aboriginal and Torres Strait Islander peoples have rights to the land—rights that existed before the

British arrived and can still exist today. Unfortunately Eddie Mabo died five months before the decision but the gigantic boost his victory provided to his people will live on for eternity.

On 26 September 1992, my Aboriginal brother Peter Matera, the West Coast Eagles speedster, won the Norm Smith Medal for best on ground in the AFL grand final in front of 95,000 people at the MCG, and millions on television, becoming only the second Aboriginal to do so after Richmond's Maurice Rioli a decade earlier.

On 10 December 1992, Australia's Prime Minister Paul Keating gave his iconic Redfern Address. It is still remembered as one of the most powerful speeches in Australian history, for its ground-breaking admission of the negative impact of white settlement in Australia on its Indigenous people and their society. Keating was the first Australian prime minister to publicly acknowledge to Indigenous Australians that European settlers were responsible for the difficulties they continued to face: 'It was we who did the dispossessing,' he said. 'We took the traditional lands and smashed the traditional way of life. We brought the diseases and the alcohol. We committed the murders. We took the children from their mothers. We practised discrimination and exclusion.'

Many Aboriginals had made positive impacts over previous decades—boxer Lionel Rose, artist Albert Namatjira, actors David Gulpilil and Ernie Dingo, activist Burnum Burnum, tennis champion Evonne Goolagong Cawley and, dating back to our 1800s, pioneering Tasmanian outlaw Queen Truganini (she's royalty in my eyes)—all making their names both at home and overseas, but it felt to me that the early 1990s was the first time that so many exciting and varied Aboriginal people and events had risen up in such a powerful and specific space of time. Which made that day at Victoria Park hurt all the more, because among all my other emotions, I felt like a fool for allowing myself to imagine that the hardest times may have finally been behind me and my people. That is also why I was so astonished, so genuinely shocked, that a man so respected within the community as Allan McAllister would display such concrete evidence that all this progress I naively hoped had been achieved could have bypassed him entirely, or been ignored by him defiantly. Either way, I retreated back into the shell it had taken me years to emerge from, and this time I was determined to not be tricked again.

McAllister, unfortunately, wasn't alone, and in fact was underlining a long-held belief that literally questioned the humanity of Aboriginals. A belief that suggested we were closer to primates than to humans and were therefore a subspecies, not equal to white people. As the esteemed Aboriginal journalist Stan Grant has publicly and regularly spoken of, one of the original motives behind what's now known as 'the Stolen Generations' was to breed us Aboriginals out of existence.

Part of the 'plan' was that we'd 'mate' with white people, and have 'half-caste' children, who would then also grow up and mate with white people, who'd have 'quarter-caste' children, and when *those* children grew up, *their* children would be fully white and the nation would have successfully, deliberately eradicated what a thorough DNA study of Indigenous genetics at the University of Cambridge in 2016 determined to be the world's oldest civilisation.

Between the 1910s and the 1970s, many First Nations children were forcibly removed from their families as a result of various government policies. Once these children were placed in orphanages or with white families, efforts to make them reject their culture often created a deep sense of shame about being of Indigenous heritage. This resulted in a disconnection from their culture, and an inability to pass that culture on to their children. And to discourage these children from ever seeking their ancestors at a later date, the majority of them were falsely told that their parents were abusive, had abandoned them, had died, or all of the above.

This process of mass child removal left a legacy of trauma and loss that continues to affect Indigenous communities, families and individuals today. That strain of ongoing PTSD can create what we now recognise as 'generational trauma', so just as blue eyes, shyness, big feet, mathematical skills, aggression, red hair or specific sporting abilities can be directly passed on from parents to their offspring, so too can a rusted-on sense of sadness, a lack of confidence, or an inferiority complex.

It should be noted that child removal is still happening and calls to stop the latest Stolen Generations are current and ongoing.

So when people suggest that the likes of Adam Goodes, Eddie Betts, Gilbert McAdam or me should 'get over it', years after whichever incident occurred to us, they're only proving they have no idea what it feels like to be looked upon and spoken about as inferior to others, and how long the pain stays in our system.

I suggest those people listen to the Archie Roach song 'Took The Children Away' or watch the Phillip Noyce film *Rabbit-Proof Fence* to get a further feel for this aspect of our history.

If the wholesale stealing of Aboriginal children from their families hadn't been eventually outlawed, Australia might never have had the pleasure of being entertained by brilliant young emerging Indigenous musicians such as The Kid LAROI and Alice Skye, the wonderful writer/actor Nakkiah Lui, or exciting young gun AFL players such as Adelaide's Izak Rankine and Melbourne's Kysaiah 'Kozzy' Pickett.

These guys and girls from the current generation of Indigenous youth would not have existed if the Stolen Generations regime and breeding-out plans had not been banned.

Which brings me back to Victoria Park. When Kelly, the kids and I awoke at Molly Meldrum's house the next morning, I knew I didn't want to play footy ever again. Why would I? If going to your place of work involved having you and your family's lives threatened by tens of thousands of strangers, you'd be scared shitless of attending that workplace again, or you'd get another job, right? It's not like being black was something I'd said or done, which I could express regret about, and apologise for 'doing'. Being black is something I *am*. It's not like changing teams would make the problem go away either, because while I'd be changing jumper colours, it wouldn't change my skin colour.

Gilbert McAdam suffered just as much repulsive racism as I did that day, and it was *his* dad who left the ground after having to endure thousands of Magpie fans aiming such violent abuse at his son that it left him physically shaking and vomiting with fear and fury as he reached the car park. Was this what Gilbert's dad had travelled all the way from Alice Springs to experience? To be sure, the McAdams endured the same awful encounter as I did, but it's me who still gets the lion's share of the historical sympathy. What Gilbert did avoid, to a degree, was the extra avalanche of ongoing hate that the act of lifting my jumper and pointing to my skin brought down upon me.

So, after that experience, I didn't want to play at all. But we had played finals the two previous years. We'd just beaten Collingwood at their home fortress for the first time in 17 years. I was in peak form and we were expected to make the finals again, so the club wasn't keen to see me walk away. The media reported that my continued absence was about money, but it was also about generational Indigenous trauma and how this event had triggered my own. At times I became confused myself and thought more money might be the answer. So I did ask for more money, sure, during that week-long emotional roller-coaster and the club actually seemed relieved at times because they understood money as a motive. It was never only about money, but it did occur to me that if I *was* to keep playing, I'd want some danger money to do so.

How had it come to this? How did jumping off the springy bench seats of rusty old Holdens to take speckies on my brothers' backs on the reserve back in Pingelly lead to me being curled up at home in a quivering foetal ball four games into the season, drinking wine from the bottle in bed during the day?

It wasn't the first time we'd been abused at Victoria Park, but it was the worst, by a billion miles. Previously, various Collingwood players had said some disgraceful stuff, but in the notorious 1993 match it appeared to be the crowd's job alone.

In the days after that game at Victoria Park, a fellow Indigenous player introduced me to a man who'd recently become his accountant. This player had my best interests at heart, but the other bloke, well, let's just say I was in a vulnerable position and I'm not sure if he was genuinely trying to help, take advantage of me or exploit the St Kilda Football Club. Either way I'm responsible for myself, I accept that, but I was happy to have somebody take control of any aspect of my life because I was in a hole and struggling to climb out of it. I already had a manager, Peter Jess, who was doing an incredible job of looking after me and navigating my consistent inconsistencies. I'm not sure why I also thought I needed a new accountant. I was on $120,000 a year and this new accountant, representing me while I remained depressed in bed, asked for $650,000 a year for three seasons. He quickly watered it down to $280,000 a year. It didn't hurt that I was the early Brownlow Medal favourite after playing what were considered to be three best-on-ground games to open the season. That fourth game, in spite of the racist abuse, saw me get two votes in the Brownlow, with Gilbert McAdam deservedly getting the three votes.

So the combination of my career-best form, the team having won three games in a row, the Saints losing the next two games without me (I'm not saying my absence was the reason we lost those games, I'm just painting the whole picture) and the genuine possibility I might give the game away, was all an opportunity this accountant was looking to make the most of. And of course, his percentage would be greater if he got me a bigger deal. He told me that my willingness to walk away from a deal strengthened his bargaining power. I was generally shitty with the world anyway and probably acting like a prick as a result, plus, yes, my suspicious mind was interested to see if the club really had been underpaying me, as it was being suggested, so I let him keep negotiating. When the giant pay-rise demands weren't met, he suggested I demand a $50,000 comeback fee and a full release from the Saints at season's end instead.

The Saints were effectively being held to ransom due to circumstances nobody could have predicted. Eventually the Saints did offer me some extra money for the season but I still didn't want to play AFL footy. Anywhere, for anybody, ever again. Would you? I could barely leave the house. I feared that opposition supporters would jump on the bandwagon at every ground after they saw how badly affected I was by what took place at Victoria Park.

Years later Adam Goodes endured what I was worried I would face, crowds capitalising on a perceived or actual weakness. But is it a weakness to fear threats to your life, in letters hand-delivered by the police? Threats shouted by the thousand, over the fence, by your fellow man?

Eventually I returned in Round 8 against Essendon. I went through the motions during that game, playing well enough but nowhere near the match-winning form I'd enjoyed before all the shit had gone down. We lost that game and six of the next nine to finish 12th for the season.

It's been claimed that I derailed the team's season. That I damaged team morale and contributed to Ken Sheldon being sacked at season's end. I had no quarrel then or now with Ken Sheldon and hopefully people now have a better understanding of why the events at Victoria Park affected me so significantly.

# SEVENTEEN

The man who captured the moment I pointed to my skin so memorably was photographer Wayne Ludbey. His photo features on the cover of this book.

Wayne started at Standard Newspapers in 1981 as a cadet photographer in Cheltenham, Victoria. A friend of his dad's had loaned him an Olympus camera the year before and Wayne fell in love with photography at once. His first job involved shooting nearly 30 houses a day for the real estate section before *The Age* signed him up.

Wayne flew regularly to Canberra for political engagements, and had developed a close friendship with Prime Minister Bob Hawke. Wayne managed to photograph Hawke alone in his study the day after he'd been deposed by Paul Keating, an image that up until then had been the most widely printed shot of Wayne's photographic career. He went on to cover horseracing at Royal Ascot, tennis at Wimbledon and Australian cricket tours to India, all for the *Herald Sun*, but in 1993, 12 years into his career, he'd been swept up in the seething fury of the Collingwood crowd at Victoria Park.

Wayne had worked enough AFL games to understand the mood shifts, the rhythms, the ebb and flow of how passionate crowds behave, but this was a day like he'd never known. He had a feeling in the marrow of his bones that I was the person he needed to focus on once the game's final siren had sounded. I'd kicked a goal near the end that had sealed our victory, I'd been subjected to terrifying abuse all day, and it seemed to Wayne there was something still to unfold. As we St Kilda players, euphoric after a rare win at the Magpie fortress, collectively approached our players' race, the intensity increased. It was then I lifted my St Kilda jumper and pointed to the colour of my skin, and announced, with more authority than I've ever spoken any sentence before or since, 'I'm black and I'm proud to be black.'

While I ran into the rooms to sing the Saints' theme song loud and strong with my team-mates and wound down, Wayne was on the phone to *The Age*, arguing with Bruce Guthrie, the editor of the Sunday edition, about how this iconic moment simply had to be published on the front page. Wayne's mate, the football editor Nick Place, joined in, and they succeeded in convincing their bosses.

The photograph was printed with the headline, 'I'm black and proud of it'. Over at the *Herald Sun*, their noteworthy photographer John Feder had also successfully pushed for his own shot of the same moment (albeit a more close-up version) to become front-page news, but the *Herald Sun*'s headline left out the definitive racial element, so the combined result had less of an impact. I am still extremely appreciative of and thankful for John's contribution to the legacy.

Wayne Ludbey later told ABC Radio in Perth, ahead of the 2019 unveiling of a statue honouring the gesture I'd made that day: 'It was something that wasn't normal, it was something that you weren't used to seeing, hearing and photographing on the football field. I knew immediately it needed to be recorded in the following day's *Sunday Age* on the front page. The paper was all set to print, and I made the editors change their plan. I just kept repeating the quote to the editor, Bruce Guthrie, the Deputy Editor Michael Gordon and the Sports Editor Ken Merrigan, because I knew it was so important. If you can visualise John McEnroe at his very worst on-court, that was me. I was passionately appealing to the umpire, determined the moment needed to be captured, especially in the mainstream media. Having since met Nicky and after travelling on this road behind him for the past 26 years, it's been an education. I've learnt so much from him about Indigenous culture and I need to learn more. Just recently Nicky said to me: "I really appreciate you've changed my life, but for me, I'm having to embrace possibly one of the worst days of my life over and over again.". . . I just hope I haven't ruined his life. It was quite a sobering comment for Nicky to make.'

Thank you, Wayne, for being my ally above all else, through thick and thin, along the entire pathway. You took a risk that day and our friendship has been my reward.

# EIGHTEEN

Ken Sheldon had taken us to the finals in two of his four years, becoming the Saints' most successful coach in 20 years, but after just one season without finals he was given the boot in 1993 and replaced by one of his assistants, Stan Alves. A former Melbourne captain, Alves had joined North Melbourne in time to play in their 1977 Premiership, and having been a childhood North Melbourne fan at the time in faraway Pingelly, I was pretty excited to play under him. When Ken Sheldon was first sacked, Stan had tried to quit as a show of loyalty but Ken had insisted Stan take the top job the club was offering him, which represented the man Ken Sheldon was.

I was sad to see Ken go after seven years as his team-mate or under his guidance as coach, but these decisions were above me. Ken was a funny, clever and considerate man. Ken had also invited Stan to join the coaching team shortly after Stan's son had been killed at a railway crossing.

Unfortunately, in Stan's first three seasons as coach we delivered poor results. Some of the playing list were loose cannons, including me. I'd regularly call Stan on Monday mornings, claiming some kind of illness as the reason why I'd be a no-show for training that day. Stan cleverly decided that whenever I called in sick I should come to the club where our doctors would provide me with the best possible care, free of charge. That put an end to that little scam of mine.

I also had zero interest or understanding of team meetings, or strategic discussions, and either couldn't or wouldn't absorb any of the information. My best way of preparing to play was to simply turn up and obey my instincts, but that's a hard sell in a team environment where everyone needs to act in unison. To his credit, Stan cottoned on to this, but still insisted I attend the meetings, even if I slept through them in the back row (which I often did).

I can see how my behaviour was not acceptable, and tough on a coach requiring everybody to toe the same line, but if I'd have adhered to the regimented rules and regulations, I don't believe I'd have been anywhere near as good a player.

Stan was easy to get along with during his first season in 1994, not that my state of mind had realigned in any way close to what I needed to be of real value to the team, but I didn't realise that was a fact until it was too late. Things changed when Tony Lockett accepted a better offer with the Sydney Swans during the off-season and left the club in 1995. Stan overcompensated for his earlier cool, calm approach by going absolutely ape-shit at our All-Australian defender David Grant during half-time of our first game. Stan took David behind closed doors but he knew we'd hear his tirade. He wanted us all to know that no player, no matter how good, was going to be exempt from getting his arse kicked if Stan felt it was required.

David Grant's exceptional form and his respect for the coach deteriorated after that tirade and he joined Melbourne at season's end. David was a lovely bloke who was adored by his team-mates, and so the resentment towards Stan from the rest of us grew.

Stan was in a difficult position. He had to either tolerate our bullshit (not that there was ever any bullshit about David Grant), which wasn't going to see us succeed, or lose us if he decided to be a disciplinarian. We hadn't done it on purpose but it was like we were holding Stan hostage. He was fucked whichever way he turned. He found a middle ground later that year, which led us to win six of the last nine games, coming home stronger than any other team, even though we only finished 13th out of 15 teams by season's end.

•

Despite the emotional toll the racial abuse I received at Victoria Park took on me, things didn't change. In 1995, at the MCG, during the Anzac Day game between Collingwood and Essendon, Collingwood's giant ruckman Damian Monkhorst allegedly chose to call Essendon's Michael Long a 'little black c\*nt'. Yep, there it was again. Long complained to the Essendon hierarchy and insisted the matter be taken up with the AFL. Eventually, some weeks after the incident, Monkhorst apologised.

This was just one of many similar incidents taking place across the league. Not all of them led to seismic change, but at last, on 30 June 1995, the AFL officially instituted a new rule. It was known as Rule 30: A rule to combat racial and religious vilification. It said:

> No player shall act towards or speak to any other person in a manner, or engage in any other conduct which threatens, disparages, vilifies or insults another person, on the basis of that person's race, religion, colour, descent or national or ethnic origin. Umpires are instructed to report such incidents and players found guilty shall face lengthy suspensions, whilst clubs may be liable for fines of up to $50,000 [equal to $100,000 in 2023].

•

Our captain Danny Frawley had announced that the Footscray game, our last of the season, would be his final game so Stan gave him the coaching reins and Danny's passionate pre-game speech saw tears rolling down everyone's faces, including his own. Danny spoke of how much he loved us all, and all Stan added before we ran out to start the game was, 'Today you are all going to show just how much you love Danny Frawley.'

Frawley had been my captain since I'd arrived at the club and, alongside Trevor Barker, there was no more adored and admired man at St Kilda. I personally thought the world of Danny and could never decide if he was more a loyal friend or a hilarious freak.

Danny once spent an entire week, as captain, telling us to ignore any sledging from Collingwood captain Tony Shaw as we approached the 1992 Elimination Final against the Magpies. Shaw had gotten under Tony Lockett's skin about four games earlier and Danny was determined that we ignore him and win on our skill alone. As Danny walked to the centre of the ground moments before the game for the umpire's coin toss, Shaw approached Danny with a barrage of aggressive abuse. Danny slammed Shaw in the chest but Shaw just continued. The coin was tossed and when Danny arrived back to where we were huddled together, awaiting his final instructions, he said, 'Forget everything I've said about ignoring him, I want every one of you to smash the shit out of him, and his team-mates, every time they go near the fucking ball.' Which we did, and we won. Job done.

In 1991 Melbourne Brownlow medallist Brian Wilson joined the Saints about two years past his prime (it was an impressive prime, to be fair). By his own admission, Brian did not lack confidence, on or off the field. This supreme self-love rubbed a few of us up the wrong way, especially when he rocked up one night in an extremely expensive sports car, parking it among our Commodores and utes. Danny was always pulling pranks and decided one night to sneakily superglue Brian's windscreen wipers to the windscreen, which burned them out the next time it rained. Brian waited a few weeks before seeking revenge, which he did by zipping live mice into Danny's tracksuit trouser pockets while he was out training. On the field Danny was fearless but off it he was a potato farmer who was paranoid about snakes so his immediate reaction upon feeling something obviously alive in his tracky-dacks was to repeatedly scream the word 'Snake!' in a high-pitched voice as he hilariously ran in circles and tried to pull his pants off at the same time.

Even outside the club we knew Danny was held in the highest regard, as his regular selection as fullback for Victoria in the State of Origin games showed. Former Footscray great and state team selector Teddy Whitten adored him.

Danny's spud farming family lived in Bungaree (named after a famous Indigenous explorer) near Ballarat, and he would drive the hour and a half down for training twice a week, with Plugger and our centreman Greg Burns all in the same car. Burns was a rugged midfielder who won two best and fairests and the 1983 World of Sport Player of the Year Award, which netted him ten grand from Adidas (equal to 30 grand today). Plugger would drive the boys in his panel van, which also had his racing greyhounds in it, and you could smell the dogs on them all at training. One time Plugger, who would've been 18 at the time, rocked up in a brand new SS Commodore Group 3, but within a week he'd written it off and was back in the panel van again. The Ballarat boys would run the raffle after training, rig it and enjoy the half-dozen cans prize during their trip back home. They'd always stop off at the same Ballarat nightclub, where their regular attendance brought crowds in.

Ballarat was known for breeding hardened footballers—Lockett, Frawley, Burns and the Cunningham brothers (Geoff and Daryl)—who were all men not to be messed with and I was glad to play alongside those guys, rather than against them. Danny Frawley epitomised that ethos. He was my captain, my team-mate and my friend.

# NINETEEN

Getting used to Plugger leaving the club was difficult. Sure we still had Stewart Loewe at centre half-forward with his huge hands catching every Sherrin that sailed his way, but with all due respect, as the song goes, 'There's only one Tony Lockett'. That song, a reworking of the famous Cuban love song 'Guantanamera', was a Top 40 hit in 1999, written and performed by the then lead singer of The Models, James Freud. The Seven Network played the Lockett song as a lead-up to Plugger scoring his 1300th goal to break the AFL all-time goal-kicking record.

If AFL was a sport played worldwide, Tony Lockett would be held in the same high esteem as Serena Williams, Diego Maradona and Michael Jordan. The greatest privilege of my career is to have witnessed Tony Lockett in action, from up close, on a weekly basis. Sure, I'm known to have assisted his greatness by passing the ball to him for many of the goals he kicked, as are Robert Harvey, Nathan Burke and a bunch of our team-mates, but Plugger would have found a way to be supreme without us (and did so when he went to Sydney). I'm just happy to think I may have made it a little easier for him to display his astronomical abilities.

Tony Lockett was the strongest player I've ever seen, the fastest player over the first 10 metres and the most accurate kick for goal, with the most simple kicking style. His minimalist approach to goal-kicking would make a biomechanic weep in wonder. He could beat his opponent when the ball was in the air or when it was on the ground. He could beat three or four opponents at any one time. I used to think that if the footy was kicked in the air towards Plugger and it was just him versus the opposition's entire 18 players, then he would still mark that ball. He could mark the ball two-handed or one-handed, in front of his face, over his head, on his chest, diving forwards or diving sideways, in the dry or in the wet, on the run or standing still. And he was impossible to tackle. As a person he was (and still is) loyal, hardworking, friendly, clever and funny. But he's mainly shy until he knows you well.

You might get the impression that I love the man, and you'd be right. His other attribute, if that's the word, was his anger. If Tony Lockett believed his direct opponent was cheating, by illegally holding his arms or his jumper, he'd usually warn them once, before hurting them physically if they tried that shit again. Being a full-forward, his team's main attacking option, his opponents were fullbacks, who are usually among the two or three biggest, strongest players in any side. But if Plugger decided to get them in a headlock during a wrestle, I'd fear for their lives. North Melbourne's Mick Martyn, Footscray's Ricky Kennedy and Guy McKenna of the West Coast Eagles were three of the toughest men I ever saw play the game, but none of them stood a chance if it got nasty with Plugger. He was indestructible. He was combustible. If you caught him on a bad day, and breaking the rules was how you intended to beat him, you'd probably regret it. Playing by the rules rarely beat Plugger, so breaking the rules was often the only option. Plugger's 1360 goals (the most ever kicked) in 281 games, at 4.84 goals a game, pretty much prove that nobody found a way to get the better of him. Plugger kicked 66 per cent (898) of his 1360 goals at St Kilda, during 183 games.

Most full-forwards were subject to bullying and intimidation by fullbacks. Poor Sydney Swans star Warwick Capper, who people often forget was a brilliant player for three or four seasons, was a pacifist who would've been given at least one full-blooded punch in the head for every goal he kicked . . . and he kicked 100 one year.

Tony Lockett was a different breed. I remember we played Hawthorn at Moorabbin one year and towards the end of a cold, wet, muddy day, Plugger was too tired to lead for the ball anymore. It was the last quarter and, as I burst out of the centre square in possession of the ball, he beckoned me to kick it high to him in the goal square. As my kick headed in his direction, Plugger's immediate opponent, champion Hawks defender Chris Langford, was joined by his dual Norm Smith medallist, multi-premiership winning team-mate Gary Ayres (whose nickname was 'Conan' due to his physique). Two against one. As the ball reached the three of them they were joined at the last moment by the Hawks' similarly talented centre half-back, Chris Mew. Three against one. While all three muscular, experienced, talented opponents tried to push and shove Plugger away from the action, he stood anchored in the goal square like a statue, waiting until the last moment before simply throwing both of his arms out and sending Langford, Ayres and Mew sprawling on the ground like little kittens. As they landed at his feet with shock on their faces, Plugger just raised both those immense arms straight above his head and marked the heavy, waterlogged footy with one grab. I found myself laughing out loud as I regained my breath, not just at witnessing what Plugger had done but also because he reminded me of a cartoon show about a massive robot, *Gigantor*, which I loved to watch as a kid. The show's theme song came flooding back to me at that very moment. My team-mates were looking at me with curiosity as I jogged back for the centre bounce, singing about how he was 'bigger than big, stronger than strong'.

Over time, like many a marriage, the relationship between Tony Lockett and the St Kilda Football Club started to go stale. The same thing happened to me a few years later so I'm not one to judge. There didn't seem to be any major reason, and the details don't always make sense down the track, but Plugger's generally increasing rage seemed to be permanently bubbling under the surface by the time Round 7 in 1994 arrived, when we lined up against the Swans at the SCG. He kicked 11 goals that day, including the winner, but he was trying to flatten blokes all afternoon and eventually succeeded when a young fella named Peter Caven got in his way. A full-pace collision saw Caven knocked out cold. Our ruckman Lazar Vidovic said the connection between Lockett's elbow and Caven's nose sounded like a car crash.

Plugger was suspended for eight weeks, and when the financial offers to play elsewhere became more than double what the Saints could pay, the union was officially over.

Following the Peter Caven incident, Plugger obviously knew he'd get suspended for a few weeks, so he gave us about three games' worth over the next three quarters. We were 44 points down before three-quarter time but somehow came back to win by a point. When I watched the replay later, Channel Seven commentator Peter Landy, who was one of my favourites, said, 'They've pulled off one of the most amazing victories of all time.'

The greatest professional relationship of my lifetime has been with Tony Lockett.

During games, we knew what each other was thinking as if we were twins. Sometimes we'd try to have a casual back 'n' forth kick-to-kick before training and I couldn't get the ball within 10 foot of him. It was weird, the two of us both standing still, under no pressure, in front of an empty grandstand. It seemed easy but we couldn't make it work. It was so bad one day, Plugger asked, 'You been on the bongs today, cuz?' (He was joking but little did he know it was an occasional possibility: one time I got stoned in the car on the way to a game, got the first possession of the day but kicked the ball the wrong way! But that day the answer was no.) We simply couldn't fake what we had together. In the heat of the cauldron though, in the middle of a big game, before a packed crowd, with both of us fighting off at least one opponent and each moving at full speed in different directions, my feet, from 50 metres away, could place that footy directly into his hands, landing as soft and sweet as you'd kiss a baby goodnight. And the magical feeling that such uncanny alchemy gave both Plugger and me was phenomenal.

Unbeatable. Otherwordly. Winmar to Lockett. To know your minds and bodies are in such rare harmony, and for it to come so naturally, was often almost overwhelming. I miss that version of myself. I get emotional. Not necessarily sad; often the memories make me feel elated. To be so lucky to have known what it was once like. A sense of undiluted excellence. Not many people on the planet get that chance. The sensation of firing on all cylinders, to be aware that you are operating at your unquestionable best.

Mostly I'm grateful for what I had with Tony Lockett. I dream a lot about my playing days. I dream I'm actually playing again. They're extremely realistic dreams, in which I'm running like the wind, nobody can catch me, I'm untouch-able. There's no sound. The silence is golden. The footy tingles in my fingers, it feels like I've always owned it and I always will. Plugger is leading hard from the goal square, his pace off the mark leaving even the quickest opponent behind. I caress the ball onto my boot, gauging how fast he's moving so I know how far to place it in front of him. The Sherrin and the super-star arrive simultaneously at the same perfect axis of latitude and longitude, and as the footy comes to rest in his hands, the sound gets switched back on. The crowd roars, the blood surges through my veins and I never ever want this moment to end. I wake up, smiling from ear to ear, in tears.

## Tony Lockett on Nicky Winmar

Fair to say that Nicky had a lot to do with me doubling my season's goal tally during his first season with the Saints.

Nicky is one of the truly great players you could ever wish to play alongside. Quite an incredible footballer actually. On his day, unstoppable, and even freakish, which is a term you wouldn't say too often, but he had the ability to do things that you don't see too many foot-ballers able to do. He was quite an amazing talent.

As a forward you've got to know what the players up the field are capable of. Some of them have only got one side so it's pointless leading to their non-preferred side, because your chances of a pass hitting you in the area where you need it or want it are not real good. Nicky made my job a whole lot easier.

I think the quickest way home (towards the goals) is down the middle. Simple as that.

Nicky Winmar hurt the opposition with every single disposal. Not only could he kick it long, he could kick it 5 metres off the ground, from his foot to my hands, and you knew when it was coming at you directly so you had to be ready to do him justice. He kicked the ball as beautifully as it's possible to do.

He could sit on blokes' shoulders to take the highest marks—he was an absolute superstar. He took big strides that didn't look quick to the eye but he covered the ground very swiftly and he'd be on blokes before they knew it, laying tough tackles, and bouncing back on his feet like a rubber band. His spring was so amazing he could sit on blokes' heads from two steps. And I noticed that the crowd LOVED him. Whenever he went near the ball, and especially when he got the ball, it was electric. He had something special. When he was on song, especially at Moorabbin, he lit the joint up.

Some of my fondest memories over 20 years of football are playing at Moorabbin, the last quarter, close games, the crowd going off, you knew you were a St Kilda player. They were great days, y'know, down that Grandstand end, the last quarter, the joint used to rock, didn't it? That was what footy was all about . . . a lot of great memories of great times at Moorabbin, mate, what a great ground it was.

You'd have mud up to your knees some days. That's another thing about Winmar, whether it was in perfect conditions or whether it was in shocking conditions, he excelled, it didn't matter. I knew what Nicky was capable of, and the bloke I'd be playing on would think, 'No, he couldn't possibly get the ball from where he's at to where my man is leading', but Nicky could literally do anything he wanted with the footy. Sometimes I'd be guilty of putting him under too much pressure, but he'd find a way of getting it to ya. And lace out. It was a privilege and an honour to play with him.

Wow, what an unbelievable player he was. Unbelievable. You've got me thinking now about how good it really was, y'know, they were the days, mate. The way he played, tells ya that if actions speak louder than words then Nicky Winmar's actions were better than anyone's. Nothing was better than seeing him chase down an unsuspecting opponent, then bounce back up with the ball in his hands and, bang, hit you wherever you wanted it. Or kick the goal himself. Now make sure it's a good book because you want to do him justice. And when you're talking to him next, make sure you say g'day from me, okay?

# TWENTY

In 1989 the Footscray Football Club (now known as the Western Bulldogs) was given an ultimatum by the league to either go out of business with immediate effect or merge with the Fitzroy Football Club. Lifelong Footscray fans, backed by influential supporters such as highly regarded lawyer Peter Gordon and the then Footscray CEO Dennis Galimberti (who blew the whistle on live radio, alerting Footscray fans to the plan), gained the notable support of an everyday fan named Irene Chatfield. She had uncovered a legal loophole that allowed for a club member to protest against the merger if members hadn't been consulted ahead of time. She took the club to court, putting her house on the line as collateral. A stay of execution was awarded against the merger and the Footscray Fightback Foundation was formed. The club had 20 days to raise the $1.5 million required to have its licence to play in the league restored. They managed to meet the criteria in the nick of time.

In 1990 the Richmond Football Club's debts of $1.7 million almost brought it to its knees, until a campaign named Save Our Skins dug the club out of a hole. Now they're a competition powerhouse with more than 100,000 members and three recent premierships.

In 1996 the Fitzroy Football Club folded forever, and at the end of the 1996 season a merger between Hawthorn and Melbourne looked certain until a resistance led by former Hawthorn premiership captain Don Scott raised $7 million and led to both the Hawks and the Demons surviving. Both, along with Footscray and Richmond, have since won flags.

It was in this environment that the St Kilda Football Club faced its own imminent demise in 1995. President Andrew Plympton, a man I had much admiration for, announced in June that the club had until October to raise $1.7 million or else we would cease to be. The AFL was keen to reduce the number of teams and offered a $6 million inducement to any two sides willing to merge. We'd already moved from our home ground at Moorabbin to Waverley Park, as a cost-saving exercise, but now we had to hit our supporters up for as much cash as they could cough up. Players were enlisted to doorknock, hit the phones and rattle collection tins in fans' faces before games, and consider donating as much of our salaries as we might be willing or able to offer. One player who did that, despite being offered truckloads of extra cash to join the Fremantle Dockers, was Stewart Loewe.

Stewart was more generous than me and the majority of our playing list put together, and Saints fans have him (among others) to thank for the club's continuing existence. The 'others' I speak of include club shareholders such as president Plympton and vice-president Gerry Ryan (who owned the Jayco caravan empire), all generous enough to donate a collective figure of more than $250,000 to the team they'd supported since childhood. Gerry has been the most consistently supportive, friendly, understanding and influential person in my life, alongside my parents and my brother Frank.

As a player it was a curious combo of embarrassment and excitement to plead with our fans to empty their wallets, but it was necessary if we were to avoid extinction. It was during this time that Carlton president John Elliott (who my whole family had laughed at via ABC TV's *Rubbery Figures* comedy sketches in which Elliott responded to any questions by shouting the words 'Pig's arse!') had made overtures to the Saints to see if we'd be interested in joining forces, but it seemed all Elliott really wanted was the $6 million and St Kilda's best half-a-dozen players. He offered to put the Saints logo somewhere on the Carlton guernsey but it was unlikely such a promise would ever be kept and so we quite rightly, and successfully, chose to fight for our survival instead.

Saints fans reminded us all of their undying loyalty by coming up with enough money to ensure the club's survival. Various fans, including revered radio broadcaster Francis Leach, organised their own fundraising events, one of which was a rock concert at The Palace featuring numerous bands who donated their services to help raise almost $50,000.

Fighting for our survival may have distracted the entire club from winning, or at least competing, for premierships, because we finished third last on the ladder in 1995. Team-wise it was a wasted season but I did take some pride in the fact that I'd given the year a fair crack, as evidenced by being awarded my second St Kilda best and fairest.

Otherwise, the 1995 and 1996 seasons saw the blooding of an exciting bunch of fresh young faces, many of whom would be at the vanguard of a soon-to-be Saints revival. The exciting speedster Aussie Jones, Matthew Lappin, future three-time All-Australian Peter 'Spida' Everitt, future Swans premiership captain Barry Hall, and Tony Brown (who is a great man, a great mate, and still a very important part of the St Kilda Football Club to this day), all showed early promise that saw a handful of them become legends of the game.

# TWENTY-ONE

Friday, 26 April 1996 was a terrible day for everyone associated with the Saints. It was the day Trevor Barker died. Trevor was undoubtedly the most popular player at the Saints, and had been the first to welcome me to the club when I arrived. He flew up high to take incredible marks and he got down low to tackle as hard as any player ever has. Most footballers could be described as white collar or blue collar but Barks was both. I'd like to think my own ability to take big marks, while also laying big tackles, was partially inspired by the great man.

Upon retirement he coached VFL side Sandringham to two premierships in three years, and was odds on to be the Saints' next coach whenever Stan Alves's time was up. It wasn't to be, however, as cancer took Trevor before that opportunity arose. His funeral was attended by 5000 people and before the first bounce of our next game, against the Bulldogs at Waverley Park,

50 of Trevor's beloved racing pigeons were released as a tribute. Although the Saints' best and fairest award was renamed in honour of St Kilda's favourite son after I'd won my two in 1989 and 1995, the new title was backdated, so it remains a point of pride to know that I won two Trevor Barker trophies.

•

Another sad ending in 1996 was that of the Fitzroy Football Club. While not comparable to an actual death, Fitzroy had joined the then VFL in 1897 and won eight premierships, the last one in 1944. They'd produced a triple Brownlow medallist in Haydn Bunton Sr; a talismanic presence in Kevin Murray who throughout his 333-game career won a Brownlow, was named in the AFL Team of the Century and won nine best and fairests, more than any other player in the history of the game; plus legends such as Garry Wilson and Bernie Quinlan. Since I'd joined the VFL in 1987, I'd played against stars such as Paul Roos, Gary Pert, Mick Conlan and Alastair Lynch but the club's finances and on-field results had deteriorated to the point where Fitzroy was getting annihilated week in and week out. They lost their last two games by an unprecedented total of 40 goals, before disbanding. The colours and lion logo of the club were adopted by the AFL's first Queensland-based team, Brisbane (named the Bears since their first season in 1987) the following year.

•

We lost our first game of 1997 to Hawthorn by six points. After a hard summer of training it's always a big crash back to earth when you lose that opening game of a brand-new season. Before that first game, all teams are even. The future is an open book. Four quarters later and those fantasies are over.

We backed up that first loss by losing again in Round 2, to Brisbane in Brisbane by 16 goals. Two games in and already we were on the bottom of the ladder.

I didn't play in the Brisbane game because I'd been dropped from the team for disciplinary reasons. It was the first week of April and the weather was still warm. I found myself at the Court Jester pub in Chapel Street, Prahran. The pub had a TAB and you could drink and watch the races from a window seat looking onto the street. It was a sunny day, I'd picked a couple of winners, various footy fans had bought me beers, and I had a buzz on. Within literal arm's reach out the window, some well-meaning citizen in a human-sized furry koala costume was rattling a bucket, raising funds to 'Save the Marsupials' or something similar. I'd been bantering with this koala a little bit, asking whoever was inside if they wanted to take a break because I'd love to buy them a beer. They were doing society a good service, they'd been working hard and must have been bloody hot.

I only understood half the koala's side of the conversation because it was muffled, but eventually the fella came inside, removed his koala head and shook my hand. He said nobody had ever engaged him in a chat when he was working before, so if it was okay, *he* wanted to buy *me* a beer.

It was the least I could do to accept such kindness and I chose to ignore the fact that he bought the beers with money from the bucket. 'To Blinky Bill,' we said as we clinked our glasses and sipped the froth off our freshies. Ten beers later the koala's bucket was empty and we were full. Putting his head back on, the koala asked if I wanted a lift anywhere. 'Sure thing,' I said, wondering how I was going to sneak a little nap before training in two hours. I told the koala I needed to lie down in the back of his car for a minute and if he headed towards Moorabbin I would let him know where I lived as we approached the area.

Next thing I know I'm being shaken awake in Sale, two and a half hours' drive away in country Victoria. We were outside the koala's local pub and he said I should come inside because his mates would love to meet me.

'Why didn't you drop me off?' I asked angrily.

'You fell straight asleep and you were snoring with a smile on your face, so I couldn't bring myself to wake you up, mate,' he replied.

I knew my team-mates would be doing tough training drills. I noticed it had gotten very cold, my mouth was dry, and we were right outside a country pub. So in we went. I got some Elvis cranked up on the jukebox and soon the koala and I were playing doubles on the pool table, beating anyone who took us on. As darkness set in outside, I continued to quench my thirst.

Next thing I know there's a cow, an actual huge fucking cow, mooing straight into my face. *MOOOO*. What the fuck? I sat bolt upright in a bed I didn't recognise and the cow licked me on the mouth. It was obviously early morning and for a moment I had no idea where or who I was. The mooing was so loud it hurt my ears and the cow's breath stank even worse than mine must have.

I spotted a bucket (which looked somehow familiar) and spewed into it. I was in a strange bedroom somewhere with a cow leaning its massive head through the window, mooing its arse off. I got up and in another room I saw my new mate crashed out on a couch with the body of his koala costume still on. At least I now had a clue what was going on. He was sleeping so hard I wondered if he was maybe dead. He smelt like a corpse either way.

The mooing was continuing nearby and when I finally got old mate to open his eyes, he put up his dukes by instinct, probably as confused by an Indigenous bloke being up in his grill first thing in the morning as I had been by the cow. It turned out that this bloke's family owned a farm in Sale but they had gone away so he was supposed to be looking after it all by himself. The cows should've been milked hours earlier and had obviously sent one of their herd ahead to try to get their drunken uncle up and at em. It was almost midday as my host cracked a cold can for breakfast and asked if I wanted one too. I politely declined and requested he drop me at the train station. I got home and slept for almost 24 hours, having not contacted the footy club the entire time.

When I arrived for training the next night, hoping that nobody had noticed my absence, I was called in to the committee room. A couple of club administrators told me that

Stan Alves was too furious to risk expressing his real thoughts about my behaviour, so they informed me I wouldn't be playing that week, and sent me straight home. But not before asking me where I'd been.

In my head I heard the answer I wanted to give, which I knew was inappropriate so I didn't dare say it out loud. Whenever I'm supposed to be serious or apologetic, even if an apology is justified, I have a childish response that ensures I almost always end up laughing instead. Which only makes matters worse. In my head, my answer was, 'Helping a mate MOOO-ve house.' Which made me laugh out loud. The more I tried to stop, the harder I laughed.

I knew I'd fucked up. I knew I'd let everyone down. I was pissed off at myself and they had every right to be pissed off with me too. Lots of people were putting lots of time, money and passion into aiming for the same team goal—a Saints premiership—and all I could hear in my head was 'MOOO-ve house'. By now I had tears of laughter in my eyes and was doubled over, struggling to breathe. They must have genuinely thought I needed a stint in some kind of institution (and they might have been right), but I knew if I tried to tell the story, nobody would believe a word. Or worse, they might believe every word. Either way, I didn't say a word, got in my car, and headed to the nearest pub. After all, I'd just been given a few days off.

Gary 'Cat' Colling played 265 games over a 13-year career for St Kilda, and as his reward upon retirement he was given the job as the Saints' player liaison man. Which meant dragging blokes out of pubs or betting shops or anywhere else they should avoid. I reckon I kept Gary in work more than any other player on the Saints' list. I am not proud of it. Replace the term 'Where's Wally?' with 'Where's Nicky?' and you get an idea of the task he faced. So while a cattle farm in Sale was beyond his Sherlock Holmes skills, it's not beyond me to acknowledge the debt of gratitude I owe the man.

Luckily, being dropped for the second round against Brisbane meant I'd avoided busting a gut in the 30-degree Queensland heat and overwhelming humidity at the Gabba. By quarter time Stan Alves was more concerned for our players' safety than the scoreboard, and resorted to rotating players on and off the bench for the entire game, in an accidental precursor to the way the game is played today. That loss sapped more than the team's energy, it took the wind out of the whole football club's sails. To Stan's credit he knew it and called an 'extraordinary meeting' at which he pointed out every individual's strengths and weaknesses, including his own. He stressed that it was early enough in the season for a new coach to take us to the finals, and if any one of us players did not have full confidence in his ability to steer us deep into September, then he would walk away immediately.

It was a big risk to take. I stood up at once and strongly stated that we players wanted him to stay. Stan thanked me, noted that it was the first time I'd ever spoken up at a team meeting for any reason, but told me it wasn't fair for one player to speak on everyone else's behalf. Stan may have dropped me the previous week but I felt that he was an honest man who was doing everything within his power to propel us up the ladder.

During the pre-season he'd brought in a fella named Ray McLean, who had just formed a company called Leading Teams that taught leadership skills. He also brought in Ted Hopkins, who'd helped win Carlton's 1970 Premiership with four second-half goals and had just formed a company called Champion Data. I couldn't concentrate on a word either of them said but my team-mates seemed to think these new voices were helpful. Both of those newly minted companies have since become a fixed part of the AFL footy landscape and it was no coincidence that their arrival heralded our surge up the ladder. McLean in particular hardened us mentally and physically. He created training methods designed to improve our resilience, the majority of which I hated but I admit they helped. (But if I ever have to do repeated time trials up and down an extinct volcano named Mount Buninyong in western Victoria again, in 37-degree heat, it will be too soon.) Dad had me doing similar stuff as a kid but back then I was too young to know better.

Us players had a 20-minute conference after which co-captain Nathan Burke called Stan in and assured him that he was our man. Stan's speech after that was one of the greatest I've ever heard. He told us we were all a family, that if we hurt, he hurt; if we failed, he failed. He cried and we cried. He spoke from the heart. Until then we knew that he cared about us, we just didn't know he cared *that much*.

I was brought back into the team for Round 3 and we beat Collingwood by seven points. It was later revealed I'd been given the three Brownlow votes for what would be the 14th and final time in my career. Once again I'd played at my best after an enforced rest.

It felt like we were back on track, but two more losses saw us entering Round 6 in second-last place. We were due to play Melbourne that round and they were last on the ladder. We were just one spot above them and destined to miss the finals for the fifth season in a row. The word in the media was that whichever coach lost the game would get sacked on the spot. We beat them by 86 points. Melbourne's president Joseph Gutnick did a mid-game radio interview in which he effectively sacked his team's coach, Neil Balme, on air.

•

My personal problems were adversely affecting my on-field performance, and Stan Alves had more than once publicly said so—'way off the mark' was one of the phrases he used about my form during a post-match press conference. I respected Stan though because he also sang my praises when I played well.

Although I'm guessing he'd have been far from pleased one morning when a carload of us players were heading to a big game, passing a joint around as we drove. We'd stopped at a red light in the right-hand lane when the front passenger happened to casually glance to their left, and spotted Stan in the car beside us. The player burst into an immediate coughing fit, unable to speak but gesturing wildly towards our coach's car. If Stan had looked to his right at those traffic lights, perhaps this book would be a whole lot different, and shorter. But maybe all he'd have seen was a Cheech & Chong style car full of thick smoke, with no individuals visible. We won that game by a fair margin, so who's to say Stan wouldn't have been handing out the Tally-Ho papers if he'd known? Apparently I played well but all I remember is staring at the seagulls all day, like Collingwood's new recruit in *The Club*. And what a movie that was!

# TWENTY-TWO

During the 1997 season I was dropped from the team again, for disciplinary reasons, again. My marriage had been faltering all year but during the season it had completely collapsed. In hindsight I have to accept most, maybe all, of the blame. Kelly and our two kids were living in Ballarat and travelling to Melbourne most weekends to see me. Tynan and Shakira would hang out with me in the rooms before games, mucking around with footies, laughing as they climbed all over me, generally enjoying themselves. I enjoyed their company and found that their presence alleviated any pre-match nervousness I might have.

Dad had been diagnosed with an aggressive type of cancer a few years earlier and he'd fought hard but it had an evil grip on him and I was consumed by the guilt of being so far away from where I thought I needed to be, which was by his side. Every time the phone rang, day or night, I jumped like a startled gazelle. I was a nervous wreck, with his impending death looming over me. Dad constantly assured me that knowing I was continuing to live my dream (and his dream too) would help him return to full health. Talking to him over the phone from the other side of the country, when it was obvious he was slowly on his way out, was an awful ongoing experience.

Leading up to Round 11, it was June and winter already. Training was cold, dark and wet, and I was emotionally unravelling. After I'd gone AWOL in 1993, following the verbally violent game at Victoria Park, I'd been approached by a group of religious do-gooders who convinced me to become a born-again Christian. At that stage everyone knew how Geelong's superhuman Gary Ablett Sr. had embraced religion to keep him on the right path. Even I knew I was headed down the wrong path, so after many approaches from this group it made sense to give Christianity a go.

Back in 1993, once my depression from the racial abuse began to abate, I returned to the club three weeks after the 'black and proud' moment, partly because I missed the camaraderie I enjoyed with my team-mates. I'd had a clause put into my contract that allowed me a certain amount of time off to pursue my religious ambitions. I was serious about such plans for maybe three weeks. In 1997, four years later, I remembered the clause when I was searching for an excuse to avoid training. My massive man-mountain team-mate Lazar Vidovic was either injured or suspended and he helped out by reminding me of my 'Christian clause'. I promptly informed the club that

I would not be training at all that week as I intended to begin Bible studies instead.

I was secretly hoping there might be something in it for me too because I was struggling to get my shit together at that point. Lazar's life was occasionally a little rough around the edges so he agreed to come along and, who knew, maybe we'd find salvation? Forty minutes into our first two-hour group indoctrination session, Lazar shook me awake and told me to stop snoring. I asked him what he was hiding under the table and he made his first confession . . . it was the form guide. He was sure he'd found a sneaky winner in the upcoming Race 5 at Flemington but we'd have to hurry if we wanted to get a bet on. Furthermore, the burning incense was making his eyes sting. We didn't know the etiquette so, just before we walked out the door, I gave the pastor a kind of curtsy. I saw Lazar salute. And that was the end of our epiphany.

At the pub where we went to place our bet (Lazar's winner didn't win), we realised what thirsty work that Bible business had been, and belted down a few too many beers. The club got a phone call and I got dropped from the team for two weeks. So did Lazar but he wasn't able to play anyway.

Maybe I was being irresponsible and selfish. Maybe I was letting the club, the coach, my team-mates and our fans down. It might have been as simple as that. Or maybe I was looking after myself the only way I knew how?

Maybe my misbehaviour was a cry for help. I don't know the answer myself but I was due to turn 32, the same age as Cats champion Patrick Dangerfield is right now as I write this sentence. Patrick has been 'managed' by Geelong for a couple of years. The term 'managed' is used now when an AFL player in the last quarter of their career might benefit from the occasional planned mid-season rest. Dangerfield has been managed three to four times a season recently, in acknowledgement of his advancing years, and to protect him so he's fighting fit come finals time.

This stuff simply didn't happen when I was playing, and there would have been outrage if it did. Was it a coincidence that my first game back after being dropped, against the Western Bulldogs in Round 13, was my second best game for the season? And what was my best game for the season? My first game back, against Collingwood, after being dropped for a week earlier in the season. Was I being punished or inadvertently protected?

It's true that I wasn't totally rested, because part of my punishment was to play in the reserves, but I barely raised a sweat in those games because they did not matter like senior games did. It's hard to stay 'up' for an entire year in any job and there's going to be days when you're mailing it in.

My worst games usually occurred in the week before I'd get myself into trouble. I wonder now if my brain was assisting my body. I noticed I'd been pulling up more sore than usual after games and my recovery was taking an extra day or two. My performance had become inconsistent for the first time too. As an elite athlete, once your form slumps you feel the pressure of expectation. I'd never struggled for more than a game or two before and I wasn't mentally equipped to handle longer periods of poor form. Dad's slow demise and returning to an empty home each night weren't helping. I was fighting with my own mind and didn't have the psychological skills to navigate the stormy seas inside my heart.

Nowadays a player in the same situation would announce that they are experiencing mental health issues or need a break and take personal leave, often without offering a specific reason, and nobody would think twice about letting that player take time to recover. Footballers want to play football, and they work hard to get themselves onto the ground each week, so if they're choosing not to do so, you can bet there's a very good reason why.

To St Kilda's credit, the club was there for me more often than not, but because I couldn't comprehend or specifically pinpoint my own reasons for being off the boil, how was the club supposed to guess what was going on? And on some occasions I might have simply felt like a lunchtime beer or two, which became five or six, then the next minute it was almost time to attend training and I was wasted. That could have been poor discipline on my part, or it might have been my way of blowing off steam, but how was anyone to tell the difference?

So there were occasions when the club felt they had no choice but to drop me from the senior side, if only to keep the other players aware that this kind of conduct could not be tolerated, whether you were the best player, the worst player, or someone in-between.

Most seasons the administration consisted only of white people so they were probably also wondering whether to take my Aboriginality into consideration. By 'my Aboriginality', I'm referring to the fact that a lot of us Aboriginal boys had (and still have) a rocky relationship with big city life, and often experience a kind of claustrophobia that can only be eased by occasionally going off the grid. Sometimes it's not even a decision but a kind of calling, where we find ourselves drawn by a geographical magnet, away from the big smoke and towards open spaces. A couple of times I recall getting into my car and just driving . . . away . . . towards . . . anywhere else. I know born-and-bred city slickers who have been known to seek the same escape, but with blackfellas that same force can be too powerful to fight off. I think this is why many Aboriginal people relate to country music, because those guys and girls sing about wide open plains, the stars at night being big and bright, the call of family from afar . . . it all resonates deep inside our systems, to the point where, sometimes, yet another game of football suddenly doesn't seem so important. Having said all that, sometimes I was just being a prick, and it wouldn't have mattered whether I was white, black or blue.

In Round 17 of the 1997 season I became the first Aboriginal footballer to play 200 AFL games. The newspapers had created a kind of race between me and Chris Lewis of the West Coast Eagles but I don't think either of us would have begrudged the other the claim to fame. As it happened, a few weeks earlier, Chris was given a seven-game suspension (allegedly for reacting to racist remarks), which allowed me to get the 200-game title, which I'll confess I'm proud of to this day. I'm especially proud considering the incredible Aboriginal footballers who came before me. I'm also under no illusions that, just because I played more AFL games, I was a better player than Geelong's Graham 'Polly' Farmer, Kangaroo heroes Jim and Phil Krakouer or Richmond's 1982 Norm Smith medallist Maurice Rioli, or any number of Aboriginals whose individual circumstances might not have allowed them to flourish to the tune of 200 games within the AFL's confines. There are also many who never ventured to Victoria to play AFL. Stephen Michael, the South Fremantle ruckman, is one of the greatest players I ever saw or played with, but despite being chased by most VFL clubs, he chose to remain in his home state of Western Australia, where his trophy shelf groaned under the weight of his awards—two Sandover medals, five best and fairests at South Fremantle, a premiership with South Fremantle in 1980, the Simpson medal, Tassie medal, 1983 All-Australian team as captain and Australian Football Hall of Fame.

Many supremely talented, hardworking and courageous Aboriginal players have since eclipsed my final career tally of 251 games, but I can always say I was the first to crack the double hundred. Hawthorn and Port Adelaide champion Shaun Burgoyne, a *quadruple* premiership player for God's sake, became the first Aboriginal player to rack up 400 games, while 300 games have been accumulated by dual premiership superstars Adam Goodes from the Sydney Swans and Essendon/Port Adelaide genius Gavin Wanganeen (also the first Aboriginal Brownlow Medal winner). Another Indigenous 300-gamer is Adelaide Crows legend Andrew McLeod, who not only played in back-to-back premierships but was awarded the Norm Smith Medal for best on ground in both of those games. The hugely talented, versatile and durable champion Michael O'Loughlin also played 300 excellent games for the Sydney Swans, but he *only* played in the one premiership—poor bastard (joking). The fact that he kicked more than 500 goals must be some consolation.

And let's not forget the stone-cold genius of Eddie Betts, perhaps the most universally loved footballer of all time. Those endearing qualities (including his wonderfully wide and warm smile) could not disguise a ruthless determination to find the ball near goals and convert from the most astonishing angles imaginable across 350 outstanding games for Carlton and Adelaide. Other brothers to have played 200 or more since I managed the milestone include Leon Davis, Jeff Farmer, Chris Johnson, Shane Edwards, Chris Lewis, Darryl White and perhaps the most charismatic superstar in the game's history, Lance 'Buddy' Franklin, who has played over 350 games.

Longevity is admirable but it is not a fixed criteria for defining greatness in a player. We saw the wonderfully agile Winston Abraham, a brother-boy from Narrogin, play 110 games across six years for Fremantle and North Melbourne, snaring a Mark of the Year, a Goal of the Year, and a premiership medal. During a spectacular three-year stint between 2009 and 2012, Liam Jurrah played the greatest 31 games the AFL has ever seen. The first Indigenous player from a remote community in Central Australia to make the big time, he won Mark of the Year in 2010, was Melbourne's leading goal-kicker in 2011, kicked 81 goals in his 31 games and displayed otherworldly skills that gave me goosebumps.

The highlight of my career would have to be running out onto Waverley Park that day as the first Aboriginal to play 200 games, with my nine-year-old son Tynan and my seven-year-old daughter Shakira, each fully decked out in Saints gear, as we burst through my special commemorative banner together. St Kilda ended up beating the Brisbane Lions by 48 points, I kicked three goals and cried as I was chaired off the ground by my team-mates. Dad cried too on the phone that night, knowing the achievement had also earned me life membership of the AFL.

Earlier that week I was photographed by *The Age* with the Aboriginal flag draped over my shoulders. For the first time I felt like I truly understood its symbolism to myself and my people. I'd heard the designer, Harold Thomas (who was a member of the Stolen Generations and the first Aboriginal to graduate from an Australian Art School), describe that the red is the ochre of his childhood, the yellow is the sun and the light that makes things grow, while the black is the colour of our people's skin. At the 1994 Commonwealth Games Cathy Freeman had created a lot of discussion by carrying the Aboriginal flag as well as the Australian national flag during her victory lap after the 200-metre sprint. At that time the Aboriginal flag was not recognised as an official Australian flag. Her act inspired me to drape it around myself as I helped promote my upcoming milestone game. By the time Cathy (one of the sweetest people you could ever hope to meet) won the gold medal in the 400 metres at the 2000 Olympic Games in Sydney, this very same display of pride in her people was seen as a uniting moment for the nation, symbolising Australia's desire to acknowledge reconciliation and celebrate Cathy's pride in her Aboriginal heritage.

That 1997 season, we finished on top of the ladder. We'd been second last on the ladder six games in, with Stan Alves being one loss away from losing his job before that victory over Melbourne, so it had been a tremendous turnaround, helped in a major way by Jason Heatley kicking 73 goals in his first season with us after an earlier three-games-in-three-years stint with the West Coast Eagles.

On Sunday, 7 September, we easily beat Brisbane in the qualifying final at Waverley Park by 46 points to set up a preliminary final at the MCG against the reigning premiers, North Melbourne. Win that and we're in the grand final.

The win over Brisbane earned us a two-week break. Despite being knocked unconscious and carried off on a stretcher in the last quarter, thanks to a heavy shirt front from Brisbane's Steven Lawrence, I headed back home to visit Mum and Dad. I was keen to hear Dad's thoughts on the Brisbane game, while assuring Mum I would do my best to stay alive against North Melbourne. Dad said she'd been in bed with a cold flannel on her forehead from the moment I got flattened until I walked through the door. If Mum had found out I was coughing up blood for days after that hit she may not have survived. Nowadays I'd have only just met the 12-day post-concussion enforced rest period criteria before the preliminary final.

•

Halfway through the first quarter of the preliminary final against the Kangaroos, we were a goal in front when North's Corey McKernan grabbed the footy near the boundary line. McKernan had been awarded the Leigh Matthews Trophy (the AFL's Most Valuable Player award), as voted by his peers, the previous year. He'd also polled the same number of Brownlow votes as the joint winners Michael Voss and James Hird, but due to a tribunal suspension during the year, he was deemed ineligible. We viewed him as one of North Melbourne's most dangerous players.

As McKernan got the ball, our ruckman Brett Cook and our bulldozing midfield champion Nathan Burke joined forces in a double-trouble tackle that hit him like two steam trains, slamming him into the deck like a sack of shit. It was the least his shoulder could do to dislocate itself. Usually a footy crowd roars for a spectacular mark or a glorious goal, but that tackle saw Saints fans explode with euphoria. St Kilda players and St Kilda fans were as one. And we meant business.

In the commentary box, Leigh Matthews took one look at McKernan's shoulder and said, 'That bone is not where it's supposed to be.' You might think it's barbaric of me to be celebrating pain inflicted upon my fellow man, but it's every man for himself out there and the tackle was within the rules. Some games, especially preliminary finals, can boil down to a last man standing situation, and we'd managed to take one of their most dangerous soldiers down. We went on to win by

31 points in front of 77,000 people and it felt *amazing*. It was a reasonably quiet game for me but I managed to kick three goals and, most importantly, we were in the grand final. A premiership was possibly one week away.

# TWENTY-THREE

The 1997 Grand Final was literally a lifelong dream come true for me. I'd gone from pretending to play in grand finals every day as a kid with my mates, to suddenly being days away from a real one. And don't forget I was born on Grand Final Day, 1965.

In a 16-team competition we'd finished 14th in 1995. Then, in 1996, we won the pre-season competition, which, while never considered to be of much worth (the games are glorified practice matches), saw our success-starved Saints fans react as if it was the real deal, especially as we hadn't won any kind of grand final for 30 years. I won the Michael Tuck Medal for best on ground that night. Tuck, the Hawthorn champion of 426 games and *seven* premiership teams, had been an on-field opponent only a couple of years earlier. It was weird because here he was now, putting a medal around my neck for playing

179

well in what was effectively a warm-up game before the real season.

I don't know how I even got a kick, let alone more kicks than most players on the ground that night because I'd joined pre-season training much later than my team-mates, after returning drastically overweight from an indulgent summer, before solving the problem by drinking only water and eating only grapes (which have a laxative effect when eaten in large quantities) for a full fortnight. That self-devised diet, combined with two weeks of hard training, saw my playing weight swiftly return to its usual 83 kilograms. My team-mates were envious and possibly pissed off that they weren't allowed or able to rock up to pre-season later and fatter than everyone else and yet still perform to the peak of their ability. I'd have been envious and pissed off too if I'd watched someone else do the same thing, but fortunately my fast metabolism and my poor punctuality aligned. The way we celebrated that pre-season premiership, you'd have thought we'd triumphed in September, such was the thirst we collectively quenched in pubs and clubs around town. Little did we know that the very next year we'd play ourselves into a bona fide grand final.

I can't speak for footballers such as Michael Tuck but my preparation for the 1997 Grand Final was not ideal. People often ask me who the best coach I ever had was, and I always say, 'My dad'. First, last and always. When I was a kid Dad would drive me 5 miles out of town to get wood from the church for the fire, then make me get out and run all the way home, while he drove alongside me. Sometimes he'd drive ahead and wait with the engine running. I'd think, 'Great, he's going to let me off the last 2 miles tonight,' but just as I reached the car he'd drive off again. If it was getting dark he'd shout out, 'Hurry up, son, you don't want the Mullee Man to get ya!' The Mullee Man was a kind of scary dude for us Aboriginal kids. Later, when I quit secondary school and joined Dad in the shearing sheds, as if a hard day's work at 14 wasn't tough enough, Dad would stop his car halfway home, or if we'd got a ride in the workers' truck he'd ask the driver to pull over, and make me run behind for the final 5 kilometres. I'd ask him why and he'd say, 'You'll find out one day, son.'

On top of that, once a week Dad would make me run up Iron Stone Hill, a 4-million-year-old extinct volcano that rises high above Pingelly, to Apex Lookout at the top. Nowadays the trail has wooden steps but back then it was raw terrain and took me an hour to reach the peak at the best of times. It was even harder coming down, with the fear of increasing pace potentially leading to a fall, but Dad would be timing me so I could be only so cautious if I wanted to achieve a personal best.

I didn't mind too much. I loved running and was good at it but I didn't realise he was building my endurance, stamina and ability to never run out of puff. It was only when I started playing footy against adults that I understood that my ability to exhaust my opponents, leaving me free to pursue the footy without obstacle, had originated from those 5-kilometre runs beside Dad's car. Not being fatigued during a game allows your mind and body to focus on the most important aspect, which is getting the footy and using it well. Every time I got my hands on the ball, I knew that I'd deprived the other 35 players of that same opportunity. Every one of my team-mates and every one of my opponents wanted the ball too. I wasn't competing with my team-mates of course, but what I'm saying is it's not easy to get your hands on the ball during the game when you're a one in 36 chance.

The next move is to make that opportunity count. To kick a goal yourself or give the ball to a team-mate in the best position to goal themselves. Kicking the ball to nobody, or to an opponent, was the ultimate sin. You'd have been better off letting a team-mate get the ball, someone who would use it more beneficially than you.

The most comfortable I've ever felt is with a footy in my hand, during a game. Some players' heart rate rises and their mind speeds up when they're the centre of attention, ball in hand, worrying what to do with it. Not me. I never felt more relaxed than when in motion, with the immediate future of that day's game in my hands. Everything became crystal clear, unfolding before me. I felt like those kids at school who could complete a Rubik's Cube with their eyes closed. I simply knew what to do.

The rest of my life was the opposite. I wasn't anywhere near as good at any other aspect of the average everyday existence. Off the field I was often confused. My dad was the only person who could help me find a middle ground. His calls helped me make some sense of city life. I loved him and he loved me and we both felt great about that fact.

So when he died the day before my first and only grand final, I'd never felt more lost.

My birthday is on 25 September.

My dad died on 26 September.

My first AFL grand final was on 27 September.

My first thought was for Dad. My second thought was for Mum. She was essentially on her own now. I thought of Frank too, but after him every thought was me, me, me. Is that selfish? Maybe. But Dad was everything to me, and suddenly there was nothing.

At some point my thoughts turned to the grand final. Should I play? Should I not? Would I play better, or worse? Would I be a help or a hindrance? If the team didn't think I was up to it, how could they possibly say so? I knew Dad would want me to play, but he wasn't the one whose dad had just died. And he wasn't the one who now had no dad to call on the phone after the game, like I always did—win, lose or draw.

Dad had been sick for three or four years after being diagnosed with cancer, among other major ailments. I thought I was prepared for the moment when the bad news arrived, but I wasn't. Not at all. The finality hit me like a tonne of bricks. Before his death there were days, weeks and months of sleepless nights as I tossed and turned in bed worrying, fearing the worst every time the phone rang, day or night. The sheer fear of *the* moment took its toll on me. As he neared the end, each conversation we had on the phone was shorter than the last. Once it was decided he needed morphine to keep the incredible pain under control, especially so he could hang in there until

Grand Final Day, he was hardly ever awake. Dad had had a lung removed by that stage and was on a respirator. I'd flown home the week before the finals and spent time with him at Narrogin Hospital, 240 kilometres south-east of Perth, where we spoke quietly as I sat at his bedside. Dad wanted me to stay with him another week. I called Stan Alves, who said he understood I was in a tough position and it was up to me but he'd love it if I could come back for the preliminary final against North Melbourne. I agreed. I said, 'Sorry, Dad, I've got to go, you'll be right. I know you'll get strong.'

We beat North Melbourne in the preliminary final, and the next day, a week before the grand final against Adelaide, Dad sent a videotaped message wishing me the best of luck. 'You've got to win this premiership for me,' he said, 'then I can go to my rest. This is the last time I'll ever coach you, my beautiful boy, so play the game of your life.'

We lost and I played poorly. I didn't know how to think, I didn't know what to do, I didn't know where I was meant to go, but I was running around in a daze for four quarters. My gauge had gone. I remember missing what should have been an easy goal from 25 metres out early on and thinking, 'Things are going to go bad here.'

I'd told Frank *not* to let me know if Dad died before the game but Mum made him do it and I was dirty on them both. The last thing they needed was the stress of me being angry on top of their own grief, but I wasn't thinking straight. Respect goes out first and foremost to my brother and Mum because they were the true Saints. They never left my side while I chased what we all hoped to be my premiership dream. Dad's premiership dream too. My love goes out to the team-mates and club officials who visited me that day and also on the night before the big game. My heart will always go out to the players I lined up alongside the next day, and to the great Cathy Freeman and Greg 'Diesel' Williams who both came to the rooms on the morning of the big match to offer their condolences.

I flew home the next day to begin what we call the 'sorry business', which is the grieving process as we say goodbye to one of our own. I hung out in Perth for a day or two on the way because I wanted to deny and avoid the frightening and deeply sad fact of my father's death. The funeral was held back a day as a result and I buried my grand final jumper with the old man. I wanted him to keep that and it helped me feel like we'd always be together. We hadn't won the grand final but I'd come a long, long way from being born in Kellerberrin and brought up on a reservation in Pingelly, a town where we Indigenous folks weren't allowed on the main street after 6 pm, living in a shack with a dirt floor and no running water or electricity. From running beside Dad's beaten-up car as a boy in the bush, to sweating it out side by side in the shearing sheds, to laughing with each other as we drank beers, to running onto the MCG as a man in front of 100,000 people on that one day in September without him watching on but hoping he was there in spirit . . . Dad had been fighting lung cancer for four long years. It must have seemed longer for Mum who was by his side day in and day out. Looking at Dad in his coffin was the most terrifying experience of my life. I can't speak for how other people deal with death, but for me it's a soul-crushing, heart-burning, almost-impossible-to-handle hell on earth.

It can be a lonely, isolating life as a black person in a white world, no matter how many people (kind and caring white people included) try to help. When the individual who has mattered to you the most, who believed in you the most, is just *gone*, never ever to return, you cannot imagine how you're going to continue living. That's how it was for me anyway.

'I love you, Dad,' I managed to whisper as I shakily tucked in that grand final jumper before they began to close the casket. I tried not to collapse as I continued, 'Thank you for loving me too. I will never set eyes on you, or hear your voice, or feel your loving hugs again, but you are my hero, my favourite person, my best friend. Farewell. Forever.'

# TWENTY-FOUR

I've never watched a replay of that 1997 Grand Final and I never intend to either. My own issues aside, we'd lost our main ruckman, the giant Serbian enforcer Lazar Vidovic, due to a wrecked knee against Port Adelaide in the final round of the home and away season. Lazar was possibly the last of the AFL's enforcers, in that his team-mates walked taller when he played alongside us, such was his physical presence (at 6 foot 7 inches and 102 kilograms) and willingness to protect his smaller midfield maestros (Robert Harvey, Nathan Burke, Aussie Jones and I were a fair bunch of ball-winners), even if that protective plan meant he had to make the opposition bleed.

Lazar and I hit it off from his first day of training at the club. It was the beginning of the 1989 summer pre-season and I introduced myself, knowing a friendly welcome on your first day is always appreciated. I told Lazar I'd only just made it to training in time after driving all the way from Perth.

'Woah!' he said. 'You could obviously do with a stretch then right?'

'Yeah,' I replied, 'but it's going to take me longer to recover from the fright.'

'The fright?'

'At one point during the drive I saw a hitchhiker on the side of the road, in the middle of nowhere, by this bunch of dry old bushes. So I pulled over, and before he got in the car he dragged this huge, heavy sports bag from behind the bushes and hefted it with a massive effort onto the back seat. He got in beside me, puffing and sweating profusely. We took off, and after a few minutes he hadn't said anything, so eventually I held my hand out and said, "I'm Nicky anyway, mate. And your name is?" The bloke said, "None of your fucking business."'

Lazar said, 'Are you shitting me?'

'Nope. So we drove a few more miles and I was obviously now pretty suss on this fella. When we approached a road sign pointing out how many miles to various places ahead, I said, "So where are you headed?" Again, the bloke said, "None of your fucking business."'

'Jesus Christ!'

'I know, right? So by now I was thinking I could be in a bit of trouble here.'

Lazar said, 'Fucken oath, mate.'

'I spotted a service station in the distance and I pulled in and said that I needed some fuel. I didn't need fuel but I needed some thinking time, in a place where there were other people around. I still had my seatbelt on, I was looking for my wallet, my mind was going flat chat, and then the bloke just got out and walked towards the toilets. So I thought, "Fuck this." I started her up and accelerated the fuck away, leaving an actual cloud of dust behind me.'

Lazar looked at me.

I looked at Lazar.

Lazar said, 'So what was in the bag?'

And I said, 'None of your fucking business.'

If I've ever got a bigger laugh in my life than when Lazar realised I'd set him up and he'd been sucked in, then I can't remember it.

Six days after Lazar went down with his busted knee, Peter 'Spida' Everitt, our next best ruckman (who was also more than handy resting in attack), got crunched by champion Lions defender Darryl White during our victory against Brisbane at Waverley Park in the qualifying final, and ended up with a broken collarbone.

Spida had become a brilliant player, who hadn't missed a game all year and was selected in the All-Australian team that year (alongside Harvey, Burke and Jones) so his absence was another major blow. Then, to top it all off, our brilliant pack-smashing marking machine Stewart Loewe unfortunately faced an unexpected family emergency on grand final eve, which saw him spend the entire night extremely worried and awake in hospital. So all those disasters and distractions ensured that many of our best team members were missing, either actually or emotionally, as we ran out onto the MCG for the most important game of our lives.

In the hour before we burst through our cheer squad's glorious grand final banner, everything seemed heightened to me. My senses were on full alert. The smell of the liniment was stronger. The acoustics in the rooms were sharper. The red of the Sherrins was brighter. Out on the ground I saw the famous soprano singer Marina Prior. 'What the hell is she doing out on the ground?' I wondered, but then she started singing the national anthem and everything made sense again. My heartbeat slowed down to a simmer. For the duration of 'Advance Australia Fair', I was as ready as I was ever going to be. It occurred to me that 14 other teams wished they could have been there that day, teams who may have worked as hard as us, if not harder, but were now watching on a TV with poor reception in a Balinese bar, or in a Vegas hotel room, or at their sister's house, or from a seat in the grandstand, or not at all. But we, this team, the St Kilda Football Club, and me, Nicky Winmar, were about to play in an AFL grand final. This grand final. As were Adelaide, but fuck them, I was having a moment.

Adelaide was missing their superstar full-forward Tony Modra (that season's Coleman medallist) and midfield beast Mark Ricciuto (both of whom were Adelaide's All-Australian selections that year), which bizarrely may have been benefi-cial to the Crows' chances because their coach Malcolm Blight replaced Modra up forward with a comparatively lightweight and barely known defender in Shane Ellen, who proved too quick and agile for our always reliable but heavyweight division full-back Jamie Shanahan.

Coincidentally, Blight and Stan Alves had been team-mates in North Melbourne's 1977 premiership-winning side exactly 20 years earlier, but that didn't earn Stan any favours from his old friend, as Blight pulled one match-winning manoeuvre after another (such as switching my sensational Aboriginal brother Andrew McLeod into the midfield after half-time, where he won the first of his two consecutive Norm Smith Medals). Blight had learned a lot from three grand final losses when he was coach of Geelong.

And all this is without yet mentioning Blight moving midfielder Darren Jarman to full-forward at three-quarter time, where he proceeded to kick an all-time grand final record of five goals (for six in total) over the next 30 minutes, in what experienced AFL journo Damian Barrett rates as 'the greatest individual quarter of footy ever played'. In summary, I suppose it might be an understatement to say 'It wasn't our day'.

My one positive memory from that grand final was seeing Aussie Jones, my 21-year-old team-mate, in just his second year, taking five bounces down the wing from half-back in the first quarter (of a grand final!), before kicking a 50-metre goal off his non-preferred foot on the run. People talk about personal highlights and team highlights but sometimes the pride and joy of watching a young team-mate excel on a big stage can be equally thrilling.

•

In 1998 I completely lost the plot in the Round 20 game against Carlton at the MCG. My direct opponent was a kid named Anthony Franchina playing his second season for the Blues. Well-meaning footy fans on the street are always asking me, 'What did Anthony Franchina do or say that day to make you go berserk against Carlton?' And they're always surprised to hear my answer: 'Nothing'. He did nothing (but beat me).

I'd had taggers sent to nullify me before, and on one occasion (just one) I was even asked to tag an opponent myself. That was Magpie star Gavin Brown, who tore me a new one. 'Tagging' is when a player is asked—or demanded—by their coach to deny themselves the pleasure they usually get from playing the game, by sacrificing their own attempts to get the ball and instead purely focus on stopping a selected member of the opposition from getting the ball. Collingwood champion Darren Millane was a player I admired immensely and I've got no doubt he would have caused me concern but I made sure I always played on the opposite side of the ground to where he was.

When I'm asked to name my toughest opponents, I can barely even *remember* any specific opponents, because I just played my natural game, every game. I played ordinary games once in a while, for sure, but I was my own worst enemy on most of those occasions.

I respect every player I've ever played against, because it's a tough game, and it can be a dangerous game, but it just so happens that no individual player ever had my measure on a regular basis over the course of my career. *That's what I told myself anyway.* I recall several sensational direct head-to-head opponents who I lined up alongside at every centre bounce, but we'd both been given a licence to play our natural games, rather than try to nullify. There were players I'd occasionally watch as if I was just another fascinated footy fan: Carlton's Greg 'Diesel' Williams, Melbourne stars Robbie Flower and Steven Stretch (and John Blakey from Fitzroy and then North Melbourne, who didn't play 359 games by accident either). Plus, the great Peter Daicos was a sorcerer with the Sherrin and could destroy a game in five minutes flat.

When it comes to opponents whose main job was to shut me down, Geelong's Steve Hocking, Melbourne's Steven Febey, Michael Gale from Fitzroy and then Richmond, and in particular Carlton's Mil Hanna, all kept me quiet at times, but part of being a successful sportsman, for me anyway, was denial. If I'd ever allowed myself to think I was beatable then I'd have been doing half my opponent's job for them. So in my mind at least, then and now, nobody ever reigned supreme over this little black duck.

However, I will concede that there was one player who definitely, undeniably got the better of me on one particular day, and that was Anthony Franchina. Admittedly, I was still shaken and shitty about having lost both my father and the grand final in the same momentous week, and I was in the midst of some private life problems, so maybe it wouldn't have mattered who my opponent was that day. Or maybe I must give credit where it's due.

Franchina had made his debut the previous year and was playing maybe his 15th game, against me, Nicky Winmar, who'd played 12 seasons and more than 200 games. He stood beside me before the game and elbowed me hard in the ribs. It stung but I ignored it. Another day at the office. I planned to put him to bed swiftly with a burst of speed or a giant leap and he'd not get near me again. Wrong. He stopped my first attempt at what would usually have been an easy possession, by impeding my path towards the footy. He didn't get the ball himself but neither did I, which was his only job, and he'd succeeded. This had happened before, but on this occasion it pissed me off. Massively. I gave him shit about how he should try to get his hands on the ball and show the crowd his skills, and he said something like, 'I don't give a fuck about getting the ball, I just give a fuck about making sure *you* don't.'

This statement sent me into a rage. It seemed against the spirit of the game. It seemed like he was playing dirty, but he wasn't. I was just in a dirty mood. And even though this kind of approach from a direct opponent was nothing new, for some reason it affected me like it never had before.

'If you can't get a kick then you don't deserve to be out here on the ground,' I said.

He replied, 'Have a whinge, bitch,' which I deserved. But I started wondering how I might actually, legally, kill this bloke. The problem with expecting footballers to stay calm is that footballers are simultaneously asked to be aggressive. It's like trying to stop a wee mid-stream: the opposing messages get mixed up in your mind. As I pushed and shoved this kid, the footy whizzed back and forth past us as if he and I were no longer a part of the game. Again, I attempted to talk sense to him.

194

'Let's both go for the ball when it comes our way again and may the best man win, okay?'

'Mate, Parko [his coach, the much-admired multiple premiership-winning David Parkin] told me that all I have to do today is annoy the living shit out of you, and that is all I'm going to do.'

By half-time I'd hardly had a kick. His plan was working. I didn't care about the game, my team-mates, or whether we won or lost. My anger towards Anthony Franchina had become a manifestation of various other issues in my life. I was also offended that a comparatively talentless newcomer (to my arrogant, erratic mind) wasn't treating me with any degree of respect. I felt like a drunk being refused entry by a bouncer at a nightclub door.

'Don't you know who I am?' I wanted to shout, or plead.

Suddenly it was halfway through the last quarter and he'd got me beat. He'd had me beat all day. I'd effectively ensured my team was a man down throughout the game by acting like a petulant child. Stan Alves sent the runner out to drag me off the field, but I told the runner to fuck off. Then I told the umpire to fuck off, then I told a number of my team-mates who were stepping in to settle me down, or straighten me up, to fuck off. I told Anthony Franchina to fuck off too and he laughed in my face, as he should have.

It was the beginning of the end for me as a footballer, and I was the only one who didn't yet know it. The kid did a great job, but I'd made it easier for him.

Around 18 months later, I'd recently retired and I saw this kid Franchina at the airport. As I approached him, he spotted me from the corner of his eye, and quickly bent down to grab his bag. Maybe he was preparing to fight? Maybe he was about to run? Or maybe I'm flattering myself. We weren't on the field now, he hadn't had time to psych up, we were civilians in a public place . . .

'YOU!' I said. 'You little fucker.'

I reached out to shake his hand with a smile I could feel splitting my face. He shook mine and seemed relieved as he smiled back and put his bag back down.

'You did a great job on me that day,' I said. 'And I did an even better one on myself.'

After that game, I was given a two-game suspension by the club for my crappy conduct, and rightly so. I missed the final two rounds of the home and away season and came back in time to play in our two finals losses against Sydney and Melbourne.

Adelaide went on to beat North Melbourne in the 1998 Grand Final, which at least confirmed that their win against us the previous year wasn't a fluke.

Our season was finished and so was my time at St Kilda.

# TWENTY-FIVE

The St Kilda teams I played with included some of the greatest players in AFL history. Robert Harvey won two Brownlow Medals and broke the record for most disposals. Danny Frawley was Victoria's State of Origin fullback 11 times in 11 years. My fearless fellow midfielder Nathan Burke was a four-time All-Australian and AFL Hall of Famer. Only Gary Dempsey of Footscray and North Melbourne had taken more marks in the history of the game than Stewart Loewe at centre half-forward (until his rookie team-mate Nick Riewoldt went on to beat that record). Trevor Barker was inducted into the AFL Hall of Fame, and Tony Lockett kicked more goals than any other player in the history of the game.

And I was no slouch myself. That's seven unarguable A-Graders, if not more when you consider the calibre of other players who threaded in and out of the team throughout my

12 years: Aussie Jones, Spida Everitt and David Grant (each of them All-Australians), Gilbert McAdam, Max Hudghton, the underrated Justin Peckett (252 games and featured at the start of the 1995 music video for 'Greg! The Stop Sign!!' by Australian band TISM: I mean what more do you want from a man's career?), plus Darryl Wakelin (later a Port Adelaide premiership fullback) and Barry Hall (who became a Swans premiership captain at full-forward, but, before that, kicked three goals for the Saints in the second quarter of the 1997 Grand Final against Adelaide to give us a 13-point lead at half-time).

Ken Sheldon, our coach from 1990 to 1993, enjoyed a winning ratio of 54.49 per cent, which is higher than that of celebrated coaches Ron Barassi, John Worsfold, Denis Pagan, Robert Walls and Paul Roos. Sure, those guys coached a lot more games than Ken did, but they never had to coach St Kilda, so that levels the field if you ask me.

At the 1998 season's end, despite taking the club to the finals two years in a row, Stan Alves was sacked, to be replaced by Essendon great Tim Watson. The new coach's first move was to sack me—well, I assume it was his decision anyway. It was like that primary-school game where you touch another kid and say, 'You've got the germs, pass em on.' I'd averaged 21 disposals per game for the 1998 season, higher than my career average of 19, but I'd been an erratic presence at the club that year and even I could see why Watson wanted to start with a clean sheet. I'd given him and the club no choice, really. I might possibly have taken petty pleasure in seeing the Saints drop four rungs on the ladder without me in Watson's first year, before dropping another six rungs to finish last in his second (and final) season as coach, but I never like seeing my beloved St Kilda struggle. I'd worn out my welcome upon Tim's arrival, and he is correctly considered to be a champion of the game, so he has my full respect and admiration.

•

Bulldogs coach Terry Wallace gave me a lifeline, signing me to play for the Western Bulldogs in 1999 and 2000. The Bulldogs grabbed me with their second pick of the draft.

I was 33 years old and entering my 13th year of AFL footy. I played 21 games for the Doggies in 1999 (including my 250th) and, although my average disposals per game had halved to 11, I kicked 34 goals, the most I'd kicked in a season for a decade. Years earlier I'd played against Terry Wallace, who was nicknamed Plough because that's what he did—he ploughed through the centre of the ground with the ball, more times than most players ever have. He was a triple premiership player and two-time best and fairest winner with Hawthorn, before defecting to Richmond for a season ruined by injury, and then crossing to Footscray where he won the best and fairest in 1988 and 1989. I knew how determined he could be, I knew he was an experienced winner, and I knew he'd be aware of how to nurse an ageing warhorse across the finish line. I was correct in every way. Terry treated me well.

Midway through the season I became embroiled in a media storm because I bailed out of a guest spot on that week's episode of *The Footy Show*. The show had been a huge hit for years and most AFL players watched it (including me), enjoyed it and got a lot of laughs out of it. As I said at the start of this book, I'm rarely comfortable when asked to do any kind of public speaking and as the date of the TV appearance approached, I started to panic. I was certain I was going to make a fool of myself and I worried the experienced hosts might hit me with heavy questions that I wouldn't have the answers to. I thought the Elvis idea of a little less conversation was my best bet.

Sometimes it can be half an hour or a fortnight or a few months before that stress subsides and I feel like maybe I'm ready to accept another media invite. Sometimes it's two hours or 20 minutes. I can never tell. That's the nature of panic or anxiety attacks. As I've also said, public speaking is usually people's number one fear, so I'm not alone. As a result of my cold feet, I was portrayed on the show that night by a white man, wearing what's called *blackface*, who pretended to be me in my absence. Many people wonder why blackface is wrong or offensive, especially to black people. Here's a simple explanation. It's because black people used to be banned from being anywhere that white people were. In a pub, a theatre, a school, a bus. We were banned. Separated from white people. Segregated. Why? Because our skin was black. White people liked our music (internationally, they'd heard spirituals being sung by African Americans in the cotton-picking fields, for example), and wanted to hear our music, but they didn't want to be in the same room as a black person. So white people would dress up as if their skin was black and perform our music to white audiences.

Some people might question me using the term 'our' when blackface was most prominent in America, but black is black and racist is racist. I also relate to the struggle of black South Africans during apartheid. Any bigotry based on skin colour is my fight too.

At one point in history the most popular entertainer in the world was a singer named Al Jolson, a white man who sang songs about being a black person, with black make-up covering his face. The only jobs black people got were as slaves. Slaves! White people would sell us to each other, for money, so we could do manual labour for them, for no money. What the fuck? This actually happened. For a very long time. In America, and in Australia, among many other countries. Australians often doubt the existence of Aboriginal slaves, and to them I say, with an aching heart, 'Google *Aboriginal workers in chains*' and prepare for the atrocious images you'll see. You could *own* an African American, or an Aboriginal, and make him or her do very hard work for you, for nothing in return. You could also kill or bash or rape the slaves, if they didn't do what they were told (or even if they *did* do what they were told), without the law worrying too much.

When these white entertainers, who'd blacken their face to perform black music, were on stage, it wasn't enough to steal our music and make money for themselves from our creativity. No. They also spoke with exaggerated versions of our accents, often dressed in clothing that was torn to shreds (like a slave), and got laughs at our expense by belittling us with racist jokes between songs. It wasn't enough for white people to force us into slavery, no, they had to ridicule and mock us in whites-only venues at the same time.

Blackface was born from slavery and racial segregation. Blackface represents this kind of barbaric behaviour and reminds black people of those terrible times and of their ancestors who endured it. Even when the actual slavery ceased, the conditions we were subjected to was barely any better. The classic Paul Kelly song 'From Little Things Big Things Grow', co-written with Indigenous singer–songwriter Kev Carmody, depicts the real-life story of an Aboriginal man named Vincent Lingiari, who staunchly led more than 200 Gurindji people—Aboriginal stockmen, domestic workers and their families—to walk off the Wave Hill cattle station in protest against atrocious housing, terrible working conditions and sparse rations as pay, provided reluctantly by the land-owner, British Lord Vestey.

On one hand I can understand how some white people who genuinely haven't heard an alternative viewpoint, in the form of a black person's perspective, might wonder what the fuss about blackface is all about. They might think that if someone wants to dress up as a Smurf, they'd paint themselves blue. If they want to depict an Oompa Loompa from Willy Wonka, they'd paint themselves orange. So basic logic suggests that to dress up as a famous black person, you need to paint yourself black. But all I am asking, from an Indigenous perspective, is to refrain from doing so in future, due to the cultural sensitivities

I have explained above. I'm not hoping to cancel people, I'm hoping to enlighten them.

If you're white and reading this, please imagine the worst thing that could possibly happen to your family, imagine that thing actually happening, then imagine how being reminded of that bad thing might piss you off. You're told to lighten up, to get a sense of humour, you're told it's just a joke, mate. But it isn't.

•

Back to my season with the Bulldogs in 1999. We finished fourth at the end of the home and away season but I lasted 45 seconds in the qualifying final against West Coast Eagles before a hip injury put me out of business, rendering us a man down. The injury was probably going to need three weeks' recovery time, so while I was due to turn 34 on Grand Final Day, my birthday wouldn't involve playing at the MCG even if the team made it through. We lost that game against the Eagles, despite going in as favourites, and then Brisbane beat us at the Gabba in the semifinal the following week. Our season was over and so was my career.

During my time with the Bulldogs I got to play alongside Bulldog greats such as Chris Grant, Scott West, Rohan Smith, Brad Johnson, Luke Darcy and Scott Wynd, plus the talented, dangerous, dynamic duo of Jose Romero and Tony Liberatore. It was an excellent experience but while I had another season to run on my contract, I knew my time had come. Succeeding, or even sustaining, a playing career at the highest level of any sport comes from your heart and your soul and your mind—and if those three aren't communicating, it's pointless continuing.

I was rapt I'd been given a chance to play AFL football at all. To end up with 251 games to my name, well, I could retire in the knowledge I achieved my dreams (except for winning a premiership, obviously).

I can't say there aren't any regrets in my life (there are plenty) but I was pleased to have come so far. I had always stood up for my rights, which sparked that show of pride for my Aboriginality at Collingwood in 1993. If I was playing basketball or any other sport, I would have done the same thing. Everyone has every right to indulge in what we are good at, and 'my moment' helped a lot of people to listen and learn about how important mixed culture is in sport, and society as a whole, and how it can succeed if we all work together.

In 1999, along with NRL player Cliff Lyons, I was awarded Aboriginal Sportsman of the Year at the National Aboriginal and Torres Strait Islander Sports Awards. The number of accolades I was accruing, either through measurable statistical achievements or the opinions of judges on awards panels, was shifting from exciting to embarrassing. They also all required me to give a speech, which as we've ascertained, is not my area of expertise.

# TWENTY-SIX

People often wonder why footballers struggle to adjust to a normal life when we retire. I remember seeing an interview with Neil Armstrong, the first man on the moon. Armstrong saw the earth from such a distance that he could close one-eye, hold up his thumb in front of his face and see our planet disappear behind it. Upon his return home, the whole experience messed with his perspective. When his wife got mad at him because he forgot to take the bins out, he tried to explain that such minor things simply do not matter in the big scheme of things. He struggled to think *anything* was important anymore. What he'd experienced was beyond most people's comprehension. Sometimes beyond even his own comprehension. What had occurred in his life was miraculous. There were times when Armstrong wondered if he'd imagined it all, worried he had gone insane, fearful his family were simply smiling as he told them his implausible, invented stories.

In my own much smaller way, I could relate. For him to walk on the moon made him a god in his world. For myself to walk on the MCG made me a god in mine. Both of us were looked up to by the general public on the streets where we lived. All senior AFL footballers (and astronauts!) have experienced, and enjoyed, this hero worship. And even if we once *were* viewed that way, in certain endeavours, well . . . that was then and this is now. But *now* isn't *then* and that's our problem.

Then there's the 'professional footballer' concept that basically began at the same time I started playing AFL. In every era before that, footballers were expected to hold down a day job. They needed to if they were to survive financially. Then, as players began to earn big money, clubs expected more in return, and as soon as one club began demanding its players spend all day every day preparing to play on the Saturday, then every other club fell into line for fear of giving that first club an advantage. What the league didn't foresee is that being a professional footballer prevented players from being a professional anything else. Beforehand, footballers were also plumbers, accountants and cops. I even remember seeing a story after school on *Simon Townsend's Wonder World* about a former St Kilda ruckman named Darryl Cowie who was a glassblower. These players weren't suddenly expected to begin living in the 'real world' once their playing days were over, because they'd never stopped working during the week. Yes, we all need to take responsibility for ourselves, and yes, I could have secured my future by taking on a profession part-time perhaps, or I could have been studying while I was playing, but when you're 23, making great money, and only need to play footy to earn it, life after football, and your own mortality, are rarely at the front of your mind. I thought I would play footy forever. I thought I would live forever. Turns out neither of those thoughts have any basis in fact.

Essendon's Paul Vander Haar and I were similar (if likening myself to Neil Armstrong was too much for you) because we'd both come back onto the field after suffering concussions in our careers, and we both enjoyed a drink during the season. In recent years, several players, including the masterly Melbourne defender Steven May, have been photographed enjoying a beer or two on their days off by members of the public and subsequently disciplined by their clubs. May was out injured at the time, so his argument was that a beer couldn't affect the way he played. May's club Melbourne, and their fans, would argue that footballers are hampering their recovery process by enjoying an ice-cold ale. Footballers today aren't allowed to relax with a beer, and we wonder why so many young blokes are suffering from mental health issues.

Being out injured is stressful. And it's lonely too. If mobile phone photography had been around during my career I would not have played ten games. The current generation of players lives in a world where everyone has a phone camera and access to dozens of internet forums on that same phone, so photos go viral almost immediately. In my playing days, 'going viral' usually meant you'd got glandular fever from pashing too many girls at a party. Sure, there's a difference between 'relaxing with a beer' and being wasted by lunchtime three days a week during the season (like I often was, particularly if I was out injured or suspended), but somewhere in-between lies a more realistic expectation of how top-flight sportspeople should be allowed to live.

I never realised how stressful it was to do your job before tens of thousands of people, all willing and able to scrutinise your every decision and criticise your every mistake. Not to mention, in my case, the racial abuse I copped every single week, both on and off the field. I don't blame myself for needing to numb all those sensations in order to survive. I wasn't as good a player as the great Gary Ablett Sr (not many were), and would not otherwise compare myself to him, but it was well known that he, like me, didn't enjoy training, often failing to turn up on time or at all, but he was still able to play as well if not better than most of his team-mates.

If nobody's being harmed and it's legal, whose business is it what way anybody prepares to play? Some might wonder how much better the likes of myself—or later on, players such as Brendan Fevola—could have been if they'd treated their bodies like a temple, but others might wonder if we'd have been lost to the game entirely if we weren't allowed to deal with the stress involved in the way we wanted. Times change and football clubs back then were willing to give certain loose units extra leeway, especially if they were exceptionally talented. I often wonder what would happen if modern-day star players such as Dusty Martin, Marcus Bontempelli or Patrick Cripps told their clubs that they didn't want to do a whole pre-season because they didn't feel like it, or if they announced they planned to enjoy four or five beers each night before bed during the season. How would their clubs react? And if their clubs said they were going to have to sack them as a result, how many other modern-day clubs would fight to allow such exceptional players those concessions if they agreed to play for *their* team?

I've been known to hit the booze too hard, for reasons I've never been able to explain. On too many occasions the bottle got the better of me. While I've been fortunate enough to never try hard drugs, the sneakiest drug of all is probably alcohol. It's the most widely accessible, it's moderately priced, and it's presented as the easiest way to socialise. The happiest TV commercials you'll ever see feature groups of people drinking, laughing, hugging and smiling. They never show people in court because too much booze is consumed on Christmas Day and a brawl kicks off.

My real addiction is the adrenaline rush and surge of super-charged self-esteem that holding a Sherrin in my hand in the middle of the MCG used to provide, knowing that all eyes are on me, and knowing I can most probably do something with that football that thrills the crowd.

That rush is simply no longer accessible to me and never will be again.

# TWENTY-SEVEN

My experience of retirement was that it is shit. Retirement from an acclaimed football career is a shit experience. I could apply a more intellectual term, with the help of a thesaurus, but I've settled on 'shit'.

The average AFL footballer's professional career lasts six years, and is over by the age of 32. A lot of people still don't know what they're going to do with their life at 32. They're only just getting started. Even a successful, highly regarded footballer who may have enjoyed a 15-year career is mostly done by 32. And if you've been lucky enough to be valued by the fans, it makes giving the game up all the more difficult. Don't get me wrong, I'm eternally grateful for every single game I was fortunate enough to play. Thankful for every kick, mark and handball. But imagine you're a postman and every time you deliver a letter to a house, thousands of people cheer. Imagine that when you deliver a very important package on a very important occasion, they chant your name. Imagine your colleagues lining up to give you high fives, fighting to carry you on their shoulders, and imagine that when strangers on the street set eyes on you, big beautiful smiles spread across their faces as they rush for a selfie, or, in the pre-smartphone days, an autograph. Imagine this happening all day, every day. Imagine being regularly in demand to appear on TV or radio shows to explain, sometimes to millions of viewers or listeners, exactly how you are able to execute those mail-delivery skills. Imagine all this adulation, across your 15-year career. I have a mate who works in middle management who says nobody ever tells him he's done a good job. Certainly his superiors wouldn't ever express gratitude for a job well done because they'd worry he might ask for a pay rise. The same mate says the only time he ever gets feedback at work is when somebody is complaining. For me, and most top-level athletes, thousands of people cheered my every move. It was an amazing experience, but you don't realise you've become addicted to it until the drug is taken away. You go from avoiding eye contact when you're out and about during your career, to quickly searching for eye contact after your career is over.

It used to be occasionally annoying to have every man and his dog wanting a piece of me when I was just trying to buy the newspaper or fill my car with petrol, even though most of them were good people saying kind things, but then I retired and it was annoying when they *didn't* want a piece of me. Suddenly, you're not just failing to make the money a high-level footballer can earn, but now you have to pay for stuff as well. When you were playing, shopkeepers would wave you away if you bought shoes or a whipper-snipper.

Initially you can barely believe this is actually happening, but you get used to thanking them and walking away (with your unexpectedly free shoes or whipper-snipper), sometimes increasing your pace as you get closer to your car in case they change their mind. Then it becomes something you expect. Then you retire and now everyone's asking, 'Cash or card?' Your superpowers have been removed and there's no guide to help you survive as a mere mortal.

(Don't get me wrong I was extremely lucky, and grateful, to have ever been given any goods or services gratis.)

Meanwhile the cold turkey of ceasing to be in the broader footy system is bringing you out in cold sweats. Anxiety attacks, chest pains, dizzy spells—they're all in high rotation as you struggle to cope with the everyday world. No more military-style daily schedule mapped out months in advance by your coaches and club administrators. No more skin-fold checks, no more beep tests, no more work clothes (jumpers, shorts, boots) being handed to you by specialist staff upon arrival at the 'coalface'. No more free massages or free food, and no more free entry to—and free drinks at—nightclubs.

Retiring from being a sports star is like a relationship break-up. Songs you've heard a hundred times before suddenly make you cry. I found myself in tears in a taxi as Paul McCartney sang 'Yesterday' on the radio, and reflecting on how I was also no longer the man I used to be.

You become scared. What's next for me? How do I create a reason to be? You regret not going to uni or getting a trade like so many club welfare officers kept telling you to do. You thought you were smart by betting on the horses or sleeping all day. Now you think you were just stupid, and as you shave while looking at the mirror each morning, you think, 'What am I shaving for anyway? A job? Who's going to employ *me*? To do *what*? For *how much*?' You used to think that when you retired you were going to make up for the years of dietary sacrifices by eating as many big fat juicy hamburgers and pizzas as you could shove into your face, but now you don't have an appetite at all. You have a thirst though. By God, you can put those beers away, because beers take the fears away, so keep em coming please.

Everything's a laugh, and everyone's laughing, and then it's daylight and you're sitting on the floor of your shower alone again, too hung-over to stand up, and the sickly sweet smell of the shampoo makes you want to spew.

You keep a wooden bowl near the front door where you chuck your keys and coins once you're home and now the bowl is filling with business cards given to you by blokes in pubs from out-of-town footy teams who'd love to chat with you about coming down to play. They don't have much money but they could lend you a car and if crowds come along then maybe they could offer you a cut of what they make at the bar? You fake interest because they're buying you beers. You're never going to come down and play. Do they think that *you*, the great Nicky Winmar, are going to play in exchange for the lend of a car and a cut of the bar, with some team based out in the back blocks of some distant suburban league?

In August 1999, before I retired, I did a favour for a friend named Tony Elbourne, who asked if I would be guest-coach of his son Nathan's local Under 12s team at training for a night.

It was a 75-kilometre drive out to Warburton in regional Victoria and I was wondering why I'd agreed to it until I pulled into the oval's car park, where I could see and smell the smoke rising from all the local houses' chimneys. I enjoyed giving the kids a few tips and, the next year, having forgone the final year of my Bulldogs contract, I decided to do what I thought retired blokes do.

I called Tony to ask if I could come stay for a weekend to go fishing in the mountains. I stayed for a week. And then I never left. Within three weeks the Warburton-Millgrove footy club had organised a car and a house for me, and in return I played for the senior team. I was still around 85 kilos and less than a year out of the AFL so it was no hardship to run around in the comparatively leisurely Yarra Valley Mountain District League.

I was pleasantly surprised to see that a lot of the fellas had skills and played with real passion. In my second game I took exception to the way my opponent was continually, to my mind, illegally impeding my path to the ball, and I whacked him. That led to a two-week suspension.

I got invited to carry the Olympic torch around Uluru in June, alongside a number of Indigenous legends—Ernie Dingo, Evonne Goolagong Cawley (I cried at the very thought of meeting her), the incredible activist Lowitja O'Donoghue, and my great mate, the glorious human that is Nova Peris (who is both an Olympic gold medallist with the Australian women's hockey team in 1996 *and* a Commonwealth Games gold medallist after winning the 200-metre sprint in 1998) among them—so the suspension did me a favour and the honour of participating on that day in Central Australia remains a treasured moment I will never forget.

In my first game back for Warburton-Millgrove I kicked five goals, and the week after that I did my hamstring. I returned to the field in form, in good time for the finals, and then, on 10 September 2000—ladies and gentleman, girls and boys, drumroll please—I won my first ever proper premiership, for Warburton-Millgrove. The Burras (who'd finished second last the previous season) finished the grand final eight points up, and I finally got to hold up a premiership cup. Sure, I'd also left the handbrake off the car the club had loaned me, and it had subsequently rolled down a hill and into the river, but in the main, playing for Warburton-Millgrove holds only great memories.

Five days after that premiership, Cathy Freeman lit the Olympic flame in the spectacular opening ceremony of the Sydney Olympic Games. Ten days after that, on 25 September 2000, she prepared for the 400-metre sprint before a capacity crowd of 112,000 at the Olympic Stadium. She won, she draped both flags over her shoulders during her lap of honour, and I was not crying, okay? There was something in my eye. And it stayed in both eyes for several hours. Cathy had provided another reminder for all Aboriginal kids that 'if you can see it, you can be it'.

In 2003 I headed back down towards Victoria's Yarra Valley region and played for Warburton's neighbouring club Seville in a tremendously enjoyable season that saw us win the premiership. My second. Well, the third if I count the 1996 AFL Pre-Season Cup at St Kilda but we'd always been taught to consider that a minor achievement compared to a real premiership cup. I came second in Seville's best and fairest behind Jason Leeds, our captain–coach.

I later played a few games here and there for a number of country teams, including Palmerston in the Northern Territory, Rutherglen in Victoria and Eaton Boomers in Western Australia. I was always made to feel extremely welcome, the people treated me well and were excited to have a famous AFL name in their midst, but my age, niggling injuries and feeling unsettled inside all ensured that I didn't stay in the one place for long.

# TWENTY-EIGHT

The St Kilda Football Club named their Team of the Century in 2003 and I was genuinely elated to be a part of it, alongside Brownlow medallists Tony Lockett, Neil Roberts, Robert Harvey, Verdun Howell, Ian Stewart and Ross Smith (the last three also played in the Saints' only premiership back in 1966), plus club legends such as Barry Breen (who kicked the point that won us that premiership), Kevin 'Cowboy' Neale (who kicked five goals in that game), Darrel Baldock, Stewart Loewe, Nathan Burke, the brilliant Trevor Barker, and big Carl Ditterich. More than 1500 players have worn the red, white and black, and I was lucky enough to be among the 22 considered the best. If the team was announced this year, I reckon they'd need to find space for at least Nick Riewoldt and Lenny Hayes. Those guys would have to fight me for my spot though, because I'm not giving it up easily.

•

Michael Long had been a truly sensational player and had also been kind enough to invite me to join him in the celebration of his Essendon team's premiership victory in 2000, of which I still can't remember a single thing. In 2004, Michael had attended yet another funeral of a relatively young Indigenous community member, which led him to believe his people, our people, had been left behind when it came to government focus. So he decided to do something about it. He announced that he was going to walk 650 kilometres from his suburban Melbourne home to Parliament House in Canberra, his goal being to speak directly with the then Prime Minister John Howard about raising awareness of Aboriginal issues and ideally working towards improving them. This became known as The Long Walk.

The walk began on 21 November, when Michael was joined by around a dozen supporters, both Aboriginal and non-Aboriginal. Five days and nights later, with hundreds of fellow Australians walking alongside him, they had walked more than 300 kilometres to Albury. The prime minister agreed to meet with Michael when he arrived in Canberra. From that discussion The Long Walk quickly became an official charity, incorporating an annual event for which Michael is joined by tens of thousands (including the actor Sigrid Thornton, who our whole family loved watching in *All The Rivers Run* and *The Man From Snowy River* when I was a kid) as they walk from Melbourne's Federation Square to the MCG, arriving in time for the start of the year's Indigenous Round 'Dreamtime at the 'G' game.

Fellow well-known and respected Indigenous folks such as the always engaging broadcaster Shelley Ware and former AFL player Nathan Lovett-Murray, who played 145 games for Essendon, make incredible efforts to spread the word to the next generation. Nathan is the great-grandson of Sir Douglas Nicholls, after whom the Indigenous Round of AFL footy has been renamed. The renaming occurred in 2016, in time to commemorate the 50th anniversary of the pivotal role Sir Douglas played in the 1967 Referendum, which recognised that Aboriginal people are citizens of Australia.

Sir Douglas Nicholls was the first Aboriginal Australian to be knighted, and the first Indigenous state governor. He played 54 games for the Fitzroy Football Club, after first training with Carlton (he was driven out by several racist officials before he could play a game for the Blues, and in 2016 Carlton publicly apologised, retrospectively, for what he'd endured). Most importantly, way back in 1938, as a leader of the newly formed Australian Aborigines Association, Doug Nicholls lobbied parliament for improved conditions for his people's population. Demanding a change to the constitution, he said:

We, representing the Aborigines of Australia, assembled in conference at the Australian Hall, Sydney, on the 26th day of January, 1938, this being the 150th Anniversary of the Whiteman's seizure of our country, hereby make protest against the callous treatment of our people by the white men during the past 150 years, and we appeal to the Australian nation of today to make new laws for the education and care of Aborigines, we ask for a new policy which will raise our people to full citizen status and equality within the community. The white people have done nothing for us whatever. Herded onto Reserves like livestock, with no proper education, how can Aborigines take their place as equals with whites? We should all work in co-operation for the progress of Aborigines throughout the Commonwealth.

It took 30 bloody years to actually achieve those changes to the constitution, and obviously plenty of commitment and patience from many people, including Doug Nicholls himself. He was known to set up a card table outside the footy and hand out leaflets while giving impromptu speeches asking people to sign the petition for a 'Yes' vote.

The 1967 Australian referendum was a huge success, and 90 per cent of Australians supported the proposal. Pastor Doug (as he'd become known by then, for his preaching to, and support of, troubled members of his community) said on TV, 'Finally, unarguably and delightful evidence that all Australians recognise Aborigines are an equal part of the nation.'

•

I was honoured in 2007 when the West Australian football commission announced an initiative in my name—the Nicky Winmar Carnival—created to provide disengaged and at-risk Aboriginal and Torres Strait Islander youths with an opportunity to reconnect with society via footy. The carnival is still in operation and it encourages disaffected kids to participate in club environments as either players, coaches, umpires, administrators or volunteers. Hopefully volunteers still get a can of Coke and Polly Waffle like I did when I operated the local footy scoreboard as a young fella!

•

The year 2008 began with Prime Minister Kevin Rudd's Apology at Parliament House to the Stolen Generations of Indigenous children who were forcibly removed from their families, a trauma my own family had lived with every day. My brother and I were lucky to not have been stolen, but the possibility of it often kept me up at night as a child. Every time we heard a car coming Mum would tell us to hide. It became an instinctive Aboriginal response, required to prevent extinction.

We wept as Prime Minister Rudd's speech both warmed and broke our hearts.

•

In August 2008, aged 37 and after 21 years playing senior AFL footy, Robert Harvey called a press conference to announce he'd retire at season's end.

Harvey amassed 5417 kicks and 3792 handballs during his 383-game career for the St Kilda footy club. That's 9209 possessions. He kicked 215 goals, won the Trevor Barker Award for being the Saints' best and fairest four times, won a Michael Tuck Medal for best afield in the 2004 pre-season grand final, won three EJ Whitten medals for being best afield for Victoria in State of Origin games, won the Leigh Matthews Trophy for Most Valuable Player as voted by his peers in 1997, won two Brownlow Medals and was All-Australian eight times. And if there was an award for loveliest fella in the game, he'd have won that every year he ever played. Harvey is a sweetheart of a human and possibly the toughest player I went into battle with. Week after week he'd get knocked around by one tagger after another (when they could catch him), game after game, season after season, and he never once retaliated. He used his skills and endurance as revenge.

The North Melbourne premiership teams of the 1990s have said that the Kangaroos spent more time preparing to curb Harvey than any other player in the competition. Harves would run 20–25 kilometres each game on average, so North would have to send a different player to him for every quarter, because no individual could last any longer against him. Harvey usually beat them all. The man was impossible to tackle (I tried plenty of times at training) and was so strong he could have probably flattened the majority of those who sought to silence him, but he only had eyes for the ball, and his heart was set on helping the Saints win at all times. Finally, as a gauge of how spectacular a player he was in 1992, Tony Lockett kicked 132 goals that year (the most he ever kicked in a season) but did not win the team's best and fairest award. Robert Harvey did. He enjoyed a beer or 12 in the off-season and was as dedicated to relaxing, when the time was right, as he was to being the fittest man in footy. Harves is also a very funny man and a highly regarded assistant coach. His last game was in a losing preliminary final against Hawthorn.

The Hawks went on to beat Geelong in the grand final the next week, after a season in which the audacious, outlandish and extravagant Indigenous megastar Lance 'Buddy' Franklin kicked 100 goals, and then on that last day in September itself, the exceptionally talented excitement machine Cyril Rioli played the game of his life, completing his debut year in the AFL with a premiership medallion around his neck. In 2015, Cyril would gain his fourth premiership medallion and his first Norm Smith Medal, emulating his dad's brother (his uncle Maurice Rioli; Richmond's 1980 Norm Smith medallist) *and* his mum's brother (his uncle Michael Long; Essendon's 1993 Norm Smith medallist).

So in the same year my former St Kilda partner-in-crime gave the game away, two of my fellow Indigenous footballers were taking the game to previously unknown levels of excellence, and so the circle of (AFL) life continued.

# TWENTY-NINE

In 2010, I went back to Pingelly for a visit and ended up staying. I was able to be close to Mum, who was 60 at the time and having lung troubles. The doctors gave her three months to live, a prediction that unfortunately proved to be correct. I should have known when I began to hear the mournful and forlorn call of the boobook owl during the night, which Noongar lore sees as a messenger of death.

Upon my return to Pingelly I felt like I drew the sight of the surrounding awe-inspiring red-orange soil through my eyes and into my bloodstream. The importance of what we call *Country*, our belief system that includes seasons of the year, animals, plants and spirits, had never seemed so meaningful to me before. I wanted to kiss the earth like the Pope kisses the ground when he lands on terra firma.

After Mum's death I was lost, in every sense of the word. I felt rudderless. Dad's death in 1997 had sat me on my arse but eventually I took comfort in still having my mum. One of the life achievements I'm most proud of is to have paid off my parents' mortgage. I believe it pleased both Mum and me in equal measure. It's what Elvis did too.

I wondered what to do now with my own life, my own future. After my AFL retirement I'd played as many years of suburban, country and interstate footy as my mind and body would allow. I felt like a shell of my former self. My daughter Shakira had just given birth to my first grandchild, named Sonni, so I drove across the Nullarbor to Victoria a few times to visit him. I still can't describe how the love I saw in my daughter's eyes for her son made me feel, or how it made me feel to hold him in my arms as his grandfather. It went deep into my soul when I recognised my own father and son in this child's eyes. We were all as one, our spirits connected directly through the Dreamtime.

I loved the solitude of the long, drawn-out drive too, seeing nothing but horizon in front of me and in the rear-view mirror, for thousands of miles and dozens of hours, 360 degrees of nothingness.

Despite the anchors of my brother back in Western Australia and my son, daughter and grandson in Victoria, my internal feelings of being unmoored would not go away. I've been nomadic; I've moved from place to place, often like a modern-day swagman. Every wellwisher who happened to set eyes on me wanted a quick chat, including people at traffic lights motioning me to roll down my car window. People would pay me compliments about my footy career or that moment I faced down a whole crowd of haters. It's a privilege to be remembered for any positive contribution you might have made to society but it can make you feel like you've been frozen in time. Like your current day self is not worthy of the adulation or the recognition your historical self earned. Every one of these quick chats also inevitably ends with the casual well-meaning question, 'So, what are you up to these days?' And I can't help but feel like whatever answer I give will be a disappointment, if only to myself.

Fifty per cent of these many daily chats will lead to me being asked to attend some kind of charity event, be it a modest local school fete or a major fundraiser for a sick child. And while I certainly rock up to my fair share of these events, and have an awareness that my attendance often pleases people, I'm rarely comfortable speaking in public. And that's aside from the fact that if I agreed to every request it would be all I ever did. I am not complaining. I'm happy people give a shit about me, but in my mind it's for who I *was* rather than who I *am*. The other problem was the 'who I am' part of the process. I've made mistakes and am in no position to preach about anything to anyone.

From Pingelly I drifted 20 kilometres away to Brookton, where my brother Frank manages a Noongar-owned sheep farm. I lived in Brookton with Beth, my long-term partner at the time, who was kind and loving and loyal to me throughout a particularly tumultuous time in my life. Whenever I was lost (literally and figuratively), Beth usually found me, for which I am both lucky and thankful. Frank's then-wife Michelle ran community programs, with meetings that I'd attend occasionally so I could try to understand various aspects of my family background. The meetings were intended to be therapeutic but I didn't seem to have the emotional tools to open up, even though I suspected it would do me good.

Frank and I often found ourselves comforting each other by the camp fire, either delighted or distraught at the wealth of memories we shared. Personal, parental, generational. Moments long gone, good, bad and ugly, never to be recaptured. We'd grieve the good stuff and express gratitude that we were rid of the bad. Some of the bad was unspeakable. Reprehensible occasions as children on the reserve when Mum and Dad placed our welfare in the hands of those they entrusted to look after us but, upon reflection, should not have (suffice to say they're demons we've been fighting to this day, and I thank you in advance for understanding that this is a topic I will not elaborate upon at any point in future).

Reflection was possible in Frank's company. Our shared tears were cathartic but with anyone else I'd shut up shop at the first sign of 'feelings'. I worried that if I started, I wouldn't know how to stop, so playing it stoic and silent was the best bet. It was the same during my playing days at St Kilda, where the psychologist struggled to hide her frustration at how incapable I was at communicating in any meaningful way, failing to understand that I was as frustrated as she was. To her it didn't seem so difficult, but equally, to me, kicking a left-foot pass at full pace to a leading Tony Lockett didn't seem difficult but it was something I'd like to have seen her try. We all have our strengths and weaknesses, for better and worse.

I helped out in the shearing sheds with Frank, like I'd first started doing when I was 14, even if it was a whole lot harder at 44 years of age after a 13-year AFL career getting crashed and bashed each week. I felt at home though, working and hanging out with my brother not far from where we were born and raised, shearing like I used to do with Dad, listening to country music in the shed on ABC Radio like we'd done with Mum in the kitchen while she cooked. It was a smaller life I was living, but a safer one too. Most importantly it was a life I had chosen. This was different from the white settlers rounding us up and designating some space the size of a footy oval as the only land we were allowed to live on. The country music was punctuated by news bulletins and I'd have backed myself to match or beat anybody in a quiz on local and international current affairs. Especially Indigenous affairs.

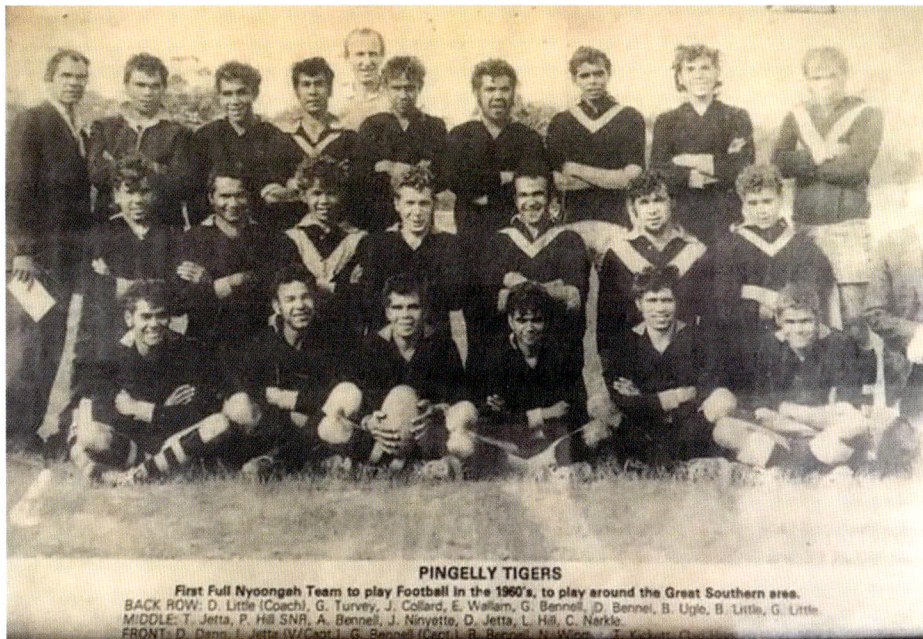

The Pingelly Tigers, Australia's first all-Aboriginal football team, founded in 1967. My dad, Neal, second from right in the front row, was a founding member. It was the cradle of so many Aboriginal AFL families: Jetta, Hill, Abraham, Narkle, Ugle, Sampi, Kickett, Bennell and Winmar.

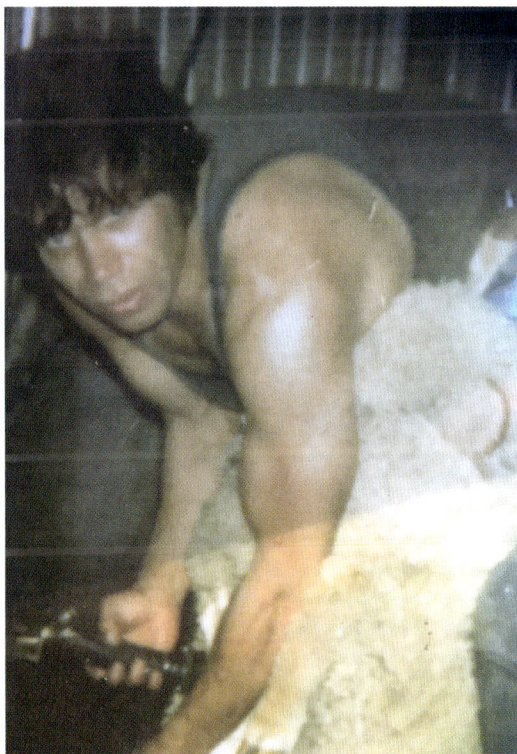

My dad at work, shearing sheep.

My mum, Meryle, and dad, Neal, on their wedding day.

Me, on the left, with my little brothers on Pingelly Reserve.

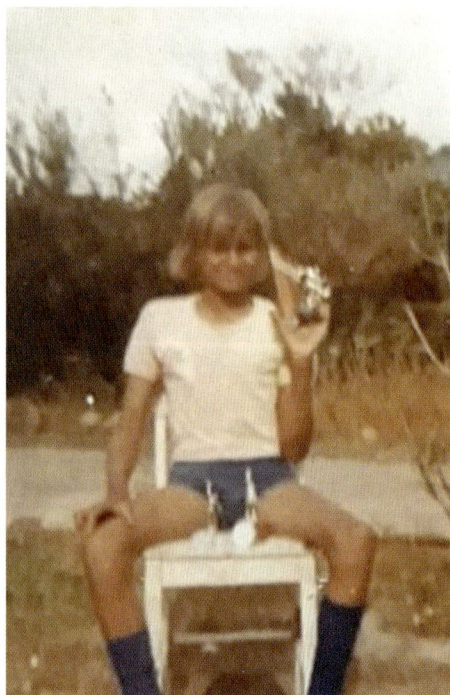

Showing off my footy trophies at 12 years old.

My first footy card photo shoot, for South Fremantle.
*Brad Gray/South Fremantle FC*

Getting my guernsey wrecked playing for South Fremantle against Claremont in the WAFL.

Iconic Saints stars assemble: Danny Frawley, Geoff Cunningham, coach Darrel Baldock, Tony 'Plugger' Lockett and some bloke named after Elvis. This was my first season with St Kilda in 1987. *News Ltd*

The King and I. We were mobbed by fans after St Kilda beat Adelaide by 131 points in April 1991—Plugger kicked 12 goals that day. We shared a special connection on the field and remain good friends to this day. *News Ltd*

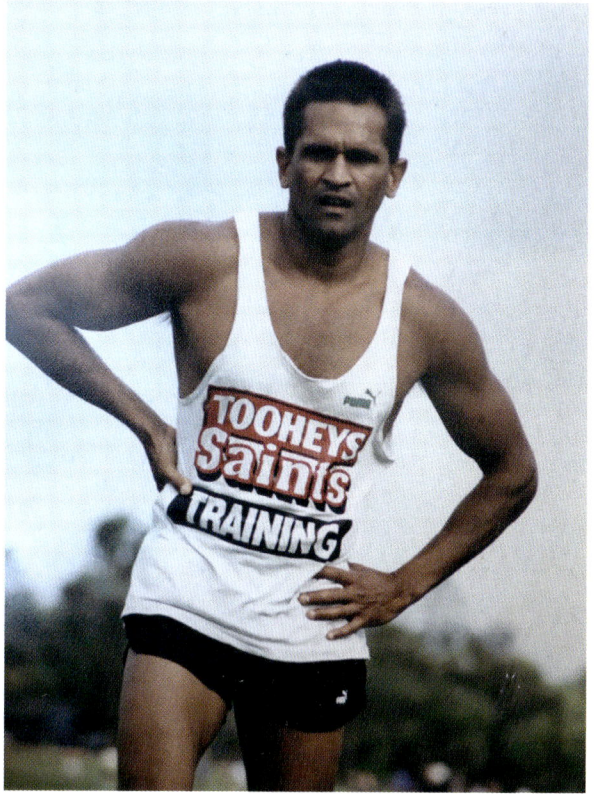

Me at training, sponsored by a beer brand. (What could possibly go wrong?)

My Aboriginal Saints brothers Dale Kickett, Gilbert McAdam and I celebrate in the rooms after winning the 1992 second elimination final against Collingwood at Waverley Park. *AFL Photos*

Pulling in a screamer against the Eagles. *AFL Photos*

Holding the 1996 Ansett Australia Pre-Season Cup. We beat Carlton by 58 points and I received the Michael Tuck Medal for best on ground.
*AFL Photos*

With my beautiful daughter Shakira after winning the Ansett Australia Cup.

With my handsome young son Tynan.

The best moment of my career: running out for my 200th game (the first Indigenous player to do so) with Tynan and Shakira in Round 17 of the 1997 AFL season. *Getty Images*

Proudly flying the Aboriginal flag outside the heritage-listed Waverley Park mosaic mural by Harold Freeman. *Michael Dodge/ Newspix*

With a keen young Saints fan named Dusty Martin. I wonder what became of that kid? *Courtesy of Dustin Martin*

You can tell that I Feel Good with the great James Brown. *David Geraghty/Newspix*

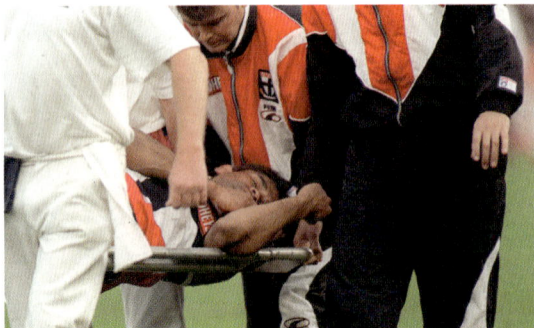

Fourth qualifying final, 1997, against Brisbane Lions. Knocked unconscious by a heavy shirt front. *AFL Photos*

A photo-op with Molly Meldrum and my team-mate Nathan Burke before the 1997 Grand Final against Adelaide. *AFL Photos*

Reaching the grand final at the MCG was a dream come true, but it wasn't to be our day. *AFL Photos*

Lining up for goal for the Bulldogs against Geelong at Optus Oval in my final season in the AFL. *AFL Photos*

I was immensely proud to be with my son Tynan during Pride Round in 2016.
*Wayne Ludbey/Newspix*

As a guest on Channel 7's *The Front Bar* with, from left, Mick Molloy, Derek Kickett, Sam Pang and Andy Maher. *David Cook/Seven Network*

Unveiling my statue in Perth in 2019: Lis Johnson, Gillon McLachlan, Mark McGowan, Louis Laumen, myself, Tanya Hosch and Wayne Ludbey.
*Will Russell/AFL Photos*

In recent years I've taken up painting as I find it relaxes me immensely. I prefer to work outdoors. This piece is titled *Nagambie Bilya*, 2022 (*bilya* means river).
*@nickywinmarart/photography by Lis Johnson*

*Winnaitch Boya* (Pumphreys Bridge), 2021. When I painted this I was thinking about my home *bilya* near Pingelly, near Pumphreys Bridge, where my family gathered for fishing, swimming, camping and telling stories. Before I was born there was a mysterious event. Small smooth stones fell from the sky like rain around Pumphreys Bridge. It happened a few times in the 1940s and 50s. My people called them spirit stones. They were warm to touch and sometimes struck Aboriginal people gently as they flew through the air. The stones rolled when they hit the ground and appeared without leaving a hole inside tents and buildings as well. I included a *djitidjiti* (willy-wagtail) in this painting. He is the spirit bird, my family's totem. He warned us about the spirit stones. He also represents me, looking back over the water, remembering my childhood. *@nickywinmarart/photography by Lis Johnson*

This triptych is titled *Green Lake Sunset*, 2022. *@nickywinmarart/photography by Lis Johnson*

My Gallipoli Art Prize–short-listed entry, *Anzac Cove, Bombardment*, 2023. *@nickywinmarart/photography by Lis Johnson*

Wayne Ludbey and I as guests on Fox Footy's *AFL 360* with Gerard Whateley and Mark Robinson. *Fox Sports*

With the record nine Indigenous players on St Kilda's list in 2022, all wearing my guernsey design. *Darrian Traynor/Getty Images/AFL Photos*

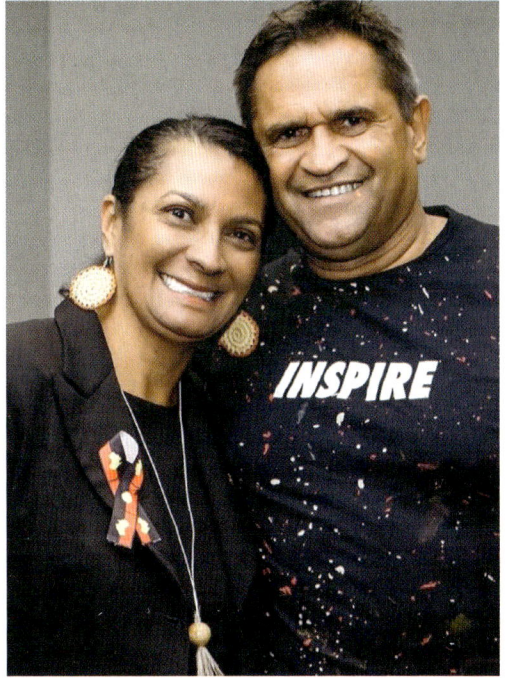

The legendary Nova Peris with a huge fan of hers at Sir Doug Nicholls Round 2022.

With my co-writer Matthew Hardy the night I was inducted into the AFL Hall of Fame.

Me being grandad to Shakira's five incredible kids. From left: Hunter, River, Sonni, Oakley and Arlia.

The *Ngarra Jarra Noun* (healing ceremony) at Victoria Park on 18 April 2023, almost 30 years to the day since I took a stand against racism on that same ground. *James Ross/AAP Image*

# THIRTY

Remember how I said earlier that when I was young I thought I'd live forever? And how mortality never entered my mind? Have you ever had a heart attack? I have and I can tell you it *hurts*.

It didn't help that I'd been working in the mines for a while, five and a half hours up the road at Geraldton, busting my balls and my back in equal measure. At my age!

I woke up at 1 am one morning in September 2012 with a rapidly escalating agony in my chest. Initially I thought the pain was just bad indigestion. I waved Beth's concerns away, thinking I'd have some milk and it would go away. But the next day, after a bad night tossing and turning, I got hit again. But this time it was the sharpest pain I have ever experienced. I've suffered bad knee and shoulder injuries throughout my football career but this level of pain topped the lot. I realised I'd better take Beth's advice and go to the hospital. The pain became so bad I worried if I might drop dead then and there as I waited for the ambulance to arrive. I'd been having dizzy spells and blackouts, which led to me falling over a couple of times, but I'd ignored them. I was obviously in denial. The incredibly alert doctor at Royal Perth Hospital took one look at me, connected me to a bunch of scary-looking machines and told me I had definitely had a heart attack.

Then he said I might well be in the middle of another one right at that very moment, so he rushed me into surgery to have a stent implanted to open up the main artery to my heart.

I was never afraid to go on the footy field—any challenge was a good challenge and I didn't usually care who I played on—but this opponent had me shaking in my boots. My body, and probably my brain, were in shock. I burst into tears a few times, I was sore all over, and after the surgery I could barely get out of bed for weeks. Again, Beth got me back on my feet.

Mortality hit me hard. My self-confidence was shot, but I appreciated that I'd been given a second chance. I was 46 at the time and wanted to make 50, at the very least, because that's the age my dear dad departed. I've since achieved that goal but not before learning some harsh lessons.

Gradually I learned to walk again but I knew I couldn't ignore the air-raid sirens. My dad was only 50 when he died due to heart disease and cancer. I had to quit smoking and cut back on booze, both of which I've always enjoyed and leaned upon. It wasn't easy.

I felt I had to speak to my people, quickly, because the

Indigenous population are nearly twice as likely to die from a heart attack as non-Indigenous people are, and twice as many Indigenous people smoke as non-Indigenous people, so while I was lucky, I wanted to forewarn others. I eagerly accepted an invite from the Heart Foundation to become an ambassador for the cause.

Back in the 1980s Yul Brynner, one of Mum and Dad's favourite actors who was in the classic films *Westworld*, *The King & I* and *The Magnificent Seven*, appeared in a commercial that young people used to mimic, especially because he had a strong Russian accent. The commercial had been filmed after he'd been diagnosed with lung cancer, although he had requested that it only be aired after he'd died. In the ad, Yul Brynner says, 'Don't smoke. Whatever you do, just don't smoke.' Now I tell people the same words.

# THIRTY-ONE

I've been the best dad I could to my son Tynan, but I wish I'd been way, way better. When my son first told me he was gay, I wasn't overjoyed. I ignorantly thought my absence from his life might have 'caused' it, and I hated myself even more than I did already (for various other mistakes through-out my life, and blows to my confidence caused by others). I was a man of my generation, and involved in an alpha-male football career where chasing women off the field as hard as we chased the footy on it was simply how we thought the whole world worked. Later on, I hated myself for thinking I was responsible for his sexual preference and for failing to realise that a homosexual life was a tougher path to tread than a heterosexual one. I mean, straight people don't fret about telling their parents which gender they're attracted to, right? 'Mum, Dad, sit down, I have something to tell you. I'm straight.'

Straight people don't ever get bashed for their sexuality by random bigots.

My generation was brought up with smash-hit VHS and cassette tapes of famous comedians doing material that seemed fine at the time, but when I look back now I realise a lot of it was homophobic and misogynistic.

Some time after Tynan told me his news, I came to my senses and realised I was as proud of my son being gay as I was proud of myself being black, and the bigotry he has faced is no different from the bigotry I have faced. And he's had to face racism too. A double whammy. I am proud of my son no matter who he's attracted to.

Since 1897, nearly 13,000 men have played AFL football at the highest level, and, so far, not one is known to have been gay. How?

Ian Roberts was regarded as one of the toughest players in the history of Australian Rugby League and he came out as gay in 1995. He was the first and, so far, only rugby league player to do so. In 2021, Adelaide United soccer star Josh Cavallo announced he was gay.

Even in a modern Australian society, which will probably (I hope) embrace whoever the first 'out' gay AFL player may be, the searing spotlight they'll undoubtedly have shone upon them (even if the response is positive) might be enough of a deterrent to keep quiet, if only to avoid becoming the token gay player.

I was pleased to help Tynan when he asked me to join him in promoting the AFL's first Pride Match, supporting and promoting gay rights, in 2016.

Tynan and I held a press conference in which I said, 'I'm proud I can do this for my son, and his friends and others out there—if you're gay, be proud of who you are. Love is love. I was proud to stand up for Indigenous people in sport and now it's time to stand up for the gay community. Life is too short.'

A year later, Australians voted in favour of marriage equality and I would love to think that Tynan and I may have helped swing a couple of those votes in the right direction.

# THIRTY-TWO

In 2019, two of the most important documentaries ever made, both on the same subject, *The Final Quarter* and *The Australian Dream* were released within weeks of each other. The subject was racism within Australian sport and, in particular, crowd behaviour towards the most decorated Aboriginal AFL footballer of all time, Adam Goodes.

Adam Goodes is one of the greatest athletes Australia has produced. He excelled as an AFL player in almost every major position on the ground. He won almost every possible team and individual trophy: AFL Rising Star Award, two Brownlow Medals, three Bob Skilton Medals (for best and fairest at the Sydney Swans), two premierships, four times All-Australian and three times Sydney's leading goal-kicker. His 372 games were the most of any Indigenous player when he retired. Adam never asked for any of these awards, but he earned them fair and square, through making the most of his talent via years of extremely hard work.

Adam also didn't ask to be named Australian of the Year, but he dived deep into the opportunity of representing his people. His acceptance speech was humble yet didn't shy away from talking about hard topics, which a lot of people didn't like. As a person and an ambassador, Adam Goodes is an all-time great.

Despite this, his fearless approach to improving the lives of his fellow Indigenous Australians rubbed some folks up the wrong way, as did the occasion when he pointed out a member of the crowd who had called him an 'ape' during the 2013 Indigenous Round game between the Sydney Swans and Collingwood at the MCG. That crowd member turned out to be a 13-year-old girl who Adam spoke to on the phone the next day.

Afterwards, during a press conference, Adam said:

I'm pretty gutted. To hear a 13-year-old girl call me an ape, which is not the first time I've been called a monkey or an ape, but it was shattering. This was Indigenous Round when we're supposed to be celebrating our culture and displaying our pride. It's not the 13-year-old girl's fault, she's so young, so innocent, I don't put any blame on her but unfortunately she's been influenced by what she hears in the environment she's been brought up in. We need to support and educate her but it felt like I was in high school again, being bullied, being called all these names because of my appearance. I didn't stand up for myself back then but I'm a lot more confident now and I decided in the moment to stand up, and I'll continue to do so. I don't want people to go after this girl though. She and her family need help and we need to educate society in general so that this hurtful abuse stops happening. The media, AFL, Nicky Winmar, myself, we're not going to tolerate racism in our game anymore.

Nathan Buckley, the Collingwood coach, added: 'The comments are unacceptable, the attitudes are unacceptable, anybody should feel comfortable to come to the footy or play footy [without being vilified].'

I could barely sit through either documentary, because they brought back a depth of recollection within my soul, which I often find is dangerous territory to explore too thoroughly. I did watch them fully, however.

What happened to me before and after my moment in 1993 started due to the colour of my skin, and escalated because I'd spoken out about it. Nothing more. I believe it was the same case with Adam Goodes.

In 2021 I took part in a documentary called *The Ripple Effect* with other prominent athletes including Nova Peris, Josh Addo-Carr, Bachar Houli and Nathan Lovett-Murray. It has powerful insights into the impact of racism in sport and elsewhere in society and should be viewed by anyone with an interest in sport. You can find a link to it at the end of this book.

# THIRTY-THREE

In May 2018, the 25th anniversary of the moment when I'd made my public statement about my skin colour, two innovative and determined advertising industry directors, Aaron Tyler and Alex Wadelton, wondered why my 'moment' had never been immortalised in bronze statue form. Wadelton had earlier written an Indigenous Round TV commercial in 2013 for the AFL. Voiced by Adam Goodes, it saw Indigenous footballers Lindsay Thomas, Shaun Burgoyne, Patrick Ryder and Andrew Walker re-enact my now memorable stance. Later, in 2020, NRL superstar Josh Addo-Carr also replicated my gesture before an Indigenous All-Stars clash against a team of Maori All-Stars. Considering Addo-Carr was born two years after my moment in 1993, I was proud of him and pleased he'd ensured that the message still resonated.

Aaron and Alex launched a crowdfunding campaign to try to make their idea eventuate. They campaigned hard, including appearances with Mark Robinson and Gerard Whateley on Fox Footy's awesome *AFL 360* show, and were rewarded when their dream became a reality. I cannot express my gratitude enough for the hard work they both did to make it happen.

I posed for the sculptor Louis Laumen and his assistant Lis Johnson (an accomplished, successful professional sculptor in her own right), and visited them at various stages of the fascinating sculpting process. Who knew how much skill, sweat and hours went into creating a statue? Louis and Lis did a truly terrific job and I loved how Lis included a subtle personal touch by adding my family's totem—willy-wagtails—to my statue's boots.

To mark the start of NAIDOC Week in July 2019, my statue was unveiled outside Optus Stadium in Burswood on Noongar land, before the 50th derby between Fremantle and West Coast. The ceremony was attended by Premier of Western Australia Mark McGowan (whose government helped fund the project), Australian Football League CEO Gillon McLachlan (who also assisted with financing), Western Australian Aboriginal Affairs Minister Ben Wyatt and the trailblazing AFL general manager for inclusion and social policy, Tanya Hosch.

Many of my family members were there, along with heaps of the greatest Indigenous players alive, including Norm Smith medallist Peter Matera, Brownlow medallist Gavin Wanganeen, genuine ornament to the game Michael O'Loughlin, the iconic Stephen Michael, David Wirrpanda, Michael Johnson, Dale

Kickett, Troy Ugle and Des Headland, among so many others of equally legendary status. And, importantly, Magarey medallist and my former team-mate Gilbert McAdam, who was on the field with me that day in 1993 and copped the same abuse. Thousands of Saints fans, and other footy fans, marched to the ceremony across Matagarup Bridge to witness the first public viewing.

Gillon McLachlan said in his speech: 'There are moments in sport that capture the public imagination and go beyond the game—and Nicky Winmar's defiant stance proclaiming his pride about his Aboriginality is one of those moments. It helped change our game, and I hope, change our country. We are very proud of this statue.'

Tanya Hosch said: 'The fact that it stands for more than football and more than just an individual, it stands for respect and stands for saying racism is not okay, is incredibly significant and I think it's still relevant today as it was then. I'm so pleased for Nicky, for the Noongar people and for Western Australia to have that recognition on Noongar country.'

In my speech, I said: 'The picture Wayne Ludbey took means a lot to me, but it means a lot to other people as well. So I can be in Queensland or Tassie, or Adelaide or anywhere, and I get stopped and people want to talk about it. Which is good. But it also makes me relive that moment. A moment when I should have been celebrating but I was dealing with racism instead. It hurts us. It always has. I don't understand it personally. Footy is for everyone no matter where you come from or who you are. Men, women, children. Black or white. Rich or poor.

This statue is for everyone. If you go to the footy or not. It's something we can all share. It's about respect. Respect for yourself, for your neighbours, your mates, your children, and as I said, respect for the person you don't know but who stops you and wants to talk.' For me personally, to have my life or any aspect of it honoured by a statue is mind-blowing. I literally cannot gather a collection of sensible thoughts to explain how it feels, even to myself.

I remain honoured to have been commemorated in such an exciting manner, but before that day, the only other Aboriginal I'd known with their own full body statue was the historical Noongar tribal leader known as Yagan, who had shamefully had his head cut off by the English in 1833. Yagan was a resistance fighter feared by colonisers as a man who fought hard to retain his people's land.

Why did he cop such terrible treatment? Yagan had killed a servant of a farmer named Archibald Butler. It was an act of retaliation after Thomas Smedley, another of Butler's servants, shot at a group of Noongar people stealing potatoes and chickens, killing one of them. The government offered a reward for Yagan's capture, dead or alive, and a young settler named James Keats shot and killed him at Upper Swan, near Perth. Yagan's head was hacked off to claim the reward. Later it was sent to London, where it was displayed as an 'anthropological curiosity' before being given to a museum in Liverpool. Yagan's head was kept in storage for more than a century before it was buried with other remains in an unmarked grave in 1964. Over the decades, the Noongar people asked for Yagan's head back. Officials exhumed the head in 1997 and repatriated it to Australia. After years of discussion on its appropriate final resting place, in 2010 Yagan's head was buried in a traditional ceremony in Belhus in the Swan Valley, near the rest of his remains, 177 years after his death.

Obviously that whole saga was reprehensible, sacrilegious and despicable, yet it's just one example of the endless reasons my people continually seek a louder voice, and need powerful people in government who'll listen to that voice. Let's hope the Uluru Statement from the Heart goes some way towards such progress.

•

While Yagan had killed a man, I assaulted one. I want to respect his version of events but my version is this: I fucked up.

I suppose I should expand a little more, but even then, the explanation is that I fucked up. And I am genuinely sorry.

I'd lapsed and was a bit pissed (as in drunk, not pissed as in 'annoyed' the way the Americans use the term) after attending a Saints game in March 2019. I had other issues at the time, but don't we all? The Saints won so I was in a happy frame of mind. My female friend and me got into the back of a taxi. The driver took one look at us and said he wanted full payment upfront. I assumed it was because we'd obviously had a few drinks but my friend thought the driver was being racist and suggesting an Aboriginal person could not be trusted. I then began to wonder if she was right. An argument started. We got out of the taxi and started walking away. The driver got out too and started shoving me. Then I got pissed the way Americans use the term. I threw punches, booted him in the bum and basically went way too far, whether his problem was with my Aboriginality or not. The court heard he was left with cuts and bruises and for that I sincerely apologise. It's not remotely acceptable. The driver recovered and I was justifiably sentenced to 30 hours of an alcohol awareness program plus 70 hours of unpaid community work.

# THIRTY-FOUR

I knew my Saints team-mate and former captain Danny Frawley had been struggling with mental health issues, but I'd also been watching him every Sunday night on Fox Footy's enjoyable and often outrageously funny weekly TV show, *The Bounce*, and listening to him on Triple M radio's show, *The Rub*. On both shows, he was as hilarious as most professional comedians. He'd become a top-flight performer on the AFL footy field, and now on TV and on radio—three varied and difficult disciplines to master, but he'd done it.

Every time I crossed his path at footy functions he'd greet me like I was his long-lost brother. He had such affection for his team-mates, even long after we'd finished playing together.

When I first heard of Danny's sudden death, even before I learned how it had come about, I burst into tears. He'd been my captain for the majority of my footy career; he'd been my friend from the day I joined the Saints. Danny had always been the life of the party and yet, somehow, beyond that external persona was a man who was also dealing with internal demons. He had been publicly open about his mental health battles and was the first person to offer assistance to anyone else enduring similar problems, but I'm not sure you can ever imagine someone you know and love actually ending their own life.

An autopsy of Danny's brain found he was suffering from low-stage chronic traumatic encephalopathy (CTE)—a form of brain disease linked to repeated blows to the head. Following the diagnosis, Danny's devoted wife, Anita, said she had 'strongly suspected there was more going on with Danny than straightforward depression'.

The St Kilda Football Club, the then CEO Matt Finnis, Danny's wife Anita and Danny's daughters Danielle, Keeley and Chelsea all collectively conceived and delivered the Danny Frawley Centre for Health and Wellbeing as a tribute to his legacy, and as an opportunity for anyone else suffering as Danny did to seek the assistance required to survive and thrive.

Danny was known by the nickname 'Spud', and in conjunction with the AFL and Movember the Saints have embarked on an annual initiative called 'Spud's Game', where, once a season, St Kilda will host a fundraising and awareness week.

Anita has recently been pushing hard for the AFL to act immediately towards protecting and compensating players who've suffered debilitating head injuries, rather than waiting years for the results of research.

The news of Danny's death meant my own mind couldn't help but rocket back to the occasion when I'd also wanted to end it all, which is a terrifying place to be.

If you are doing it tough, or think you know someone who is, don't hesitate to ask for help.

# THIRTY-FIVE

Okay so maybe you haven't had a heart attack but have you ever been knocked unconscious? I have. As you might imagine, it's excruciating. At the point of impact especially. It's also disorientating.

Being knocked out makes you feel as if you've blinked and when you open your eyes again somehow you're in a totally different place. The sky or the ceiling is the first thing you'll see once you regain consciousness. Or the concerned face of a medic, leering over you. On a couple of occasions I almost slapped that leering face, whoever it belonged to, such was the sudden shock. You kind of feel like you've come back from the dead.

Which in a way is what's happened. Your head, which contains your brain, is causing you tremendous pain. I distinctly recall one occasion, when, as I lay motionless on the ground where I'd been felled, a trainer ran out and rubbed my face with a cold flannel. Modern technology, huh? It worked though. I regained consciousness but was utterly confused. I couldn't have told you who, where or what I was.

When my eyelids snapped open, the trainer was waving his hand in front of me and asking how many fingers he was holding up. The word 'fingers' seemed familiar, as did the five sausage-y things in front of my face, but the equation wasn't adding up in my mangled mind. What fingers *were*, and what they were *called*, was not registering. The wheels were spinning in my skull but failing to gain any traction. As Dad used to say, I didn't know my arse from my elbow.

On that first occasion of unconsciousness I didn't come back onto the ground but there were other instances when I was just as bamboozled yet got brought back on later in the game. Footy teams would tell themselves anything if they needed certain affected players in the action again. The scores were close, I was one of the team's best players. We needed me out there if we were going to win. I wasn't alone; there are plenty of famous instances in AFL history where concussions were brushed off so the player could return to the field as soon as possible. When Dermott Brereton ironed out Essendon's Paul Vander Haar in their 1989 semifinal, the Essendon club doctor somehow soon decided Vander Haar was fit to come back on, leading to him swiftly striking Hawthorn's Greg Dear and getting himself suspended for three games.

Vander Haar has often stated since that he has no memory of the entire game, and in fact Essendon successfully appealed the suspension on the ground that he was concussed and didn't know what he was doing.

Somehow the appeals tribunal forgot that it was his own team's doctor who'd determined that he was not in fact concussed, before sending him back onto the ground. Once the suspension was cancelled, the club told Vander Haar he'd be playing in the preliminary final the following week but it was Vander Haar himself who had to talk them out of selecting him, due to still feeling seriously unwell. It was a different time, a different generational attitude, and we didn't have access to the medical expertise and methods of measuring the effects of head injuries that we have now.

We now know that many of the players from that era are suffering mental health complications arising from constant knocks to the head. I am one of those players. I genuinely believe I'm displaying the effects of chronic traumatic encephalopathy (CTE), and it's frightening. I suffer from dizziness, headaches and major memory lapses. I will often find myself sinking into a deep, dark state of mind only minutes after I'd earlier been having a good time.

Former Richmond champion Matthew Richardson, who played a generation after me, has spoken of his memory occasionally being wiped from one day to the next. Richo has admitted to making important phone calls to business associates, only to be told that they'd already talked the day before, but Richo had totally forgotten the conversation. Myself, I suffer from dizziness, headaches and major memory lapses. That's a joke, because I'm fully aware that I wrote those same words just a few sentences ago. Or did I?

Either way, CTE is a brain disease caused by repeated blows to the head, an ailment for which former Melbourne and North Melbourne player Shaun Smith was awarded $1.4 million in damages in 2020. Smith said his brain injury had changed his life in many ways, due to it adversely affecting his memory and mental health.

After the announcement, Smith said, 'I'm just happy that it's finally been recognised. I just hope that the AFL listens because it's people's health at risk. I've always been a pretty easygoing guy, but I was regularly getting pretty angry at the drop of a hat. Then I started forgetting a lot of things; my short-term memory especially was shot. It just goes on and on, and it doesn't make it much fun for people living around me.'

I'm scared of what the future holds, and I'm trying not to die from the stress before the side effects of repeated head injuries potentially take their toll.

Experts say players can be totally and permanently disabled as a consequence of playing football. Two independent panels of medical experts looked at Shaun's case and said the injuries caused by playing football were so significant that he would never be able to work in any form of employment again.

I can relate to everything he's spoken of. You might be reading this and thinking, 'Nicky's after his own massive payout', and I'll tell you what, if it can be proven that I am suffering permanent major problems as the result of being repeatedly injured at my place of work, and sent back into the fray while still concussed, then yes, I may well be seeking my share of compensation, especially if it's proven I was provided with an unsafe work environment.

I remember one specific occasion when I ran back onto the ground after a heavy blow and I wanted to throw up. Everything seemed to be rapidly spinning around like I was on a carnival ride.

Things haven't changed that much. A current AFL coach has been accused by a former club doctor, in documents submitted by his lawyer, of taking extreme exception after one player had suffered a concussion and a plan was devised for his recovery, including complete rest.

'Are we fucken fair dinkum,' the coach is alleged to have asked the doctor. 'Why the fuck would you change the plan when we agreed he [the player] could push through his comfort zone.'

Hawthorn's champion premiership rover Johnny Platten and his fellow Brownlow medallist midfielder Greg 'Diesel' Williams are others whose current issues with memory loss and confusion are almost certainly connected to copping numerous concussions during their playing career. When Geelong's all-time great Indigenous ruckman and my fellow Noongar man Graham 'Polly' Farmer had his brain analysed after his family donated it to the Australian Sports Brain Bank for research purposes, it was confirmed he'd suffered from CTE, the signs of which are closely related to Alzheimer's disease. The worst thing is that CTE can never be 100 per cent confirmed until the victim has died.

How can I, and lots of other former players, not be fearful that the same future might lie ahead? Every time my mind goes blank, or my moods swing erratically—both of which have recently been diagnosed by neurologists as happening more often—I worry I may be literally losing my mind.

# THIRTY-SIX

*The Marngrook Footy Show* aired its 299th and final episode in 2019, following an initial ten years on radio. There has been much debate for more than a century about the origins of Australian Rules football, with many claiming the Indigenous population created the game hundreds or even thousands of years ago, while others suggest the game was pioneered by Tom Wills (captain of the first Melbourne and Geelong football teams), who introduced the game to the 'white man'. The AFL's long-time premier statistician Col Hutchinson, together with the esteemed long-form journalist and author Martin Flanagan, both believe Tom Wills played a game called Marngrook (which means 'ball' in the Woiwurrung language) with local Aboriginals as a child, which led him to introduce the tailored version we know today as Australian Rules to his fellow white men (the inscription on the Tom Wills monument in Moyston, Victoria, as approved by his family, says as much).

Marngrook was played at Aboriginal gatherings and celebrations by sometimes more than a hundred players. For those who wondered why catching the footy from a kick is called taking a 'mark', it comes from a word meaning 'to catch', which is 'mumarki'. To support my own beliefs regarding AFL's origins, while providing balance to what could possibly be my own biased perspective, I was relieved to discover the following insight from the State Library.

William Thomas, a Protector of Aborigines in Victoria, stated that in about 1841 he had witnessed Wurundjeri Aboriginal people east of Melbourne playing the game: 'The men and boys joyfully assemble when this game is to be played. One makes a ball of possum skin, somewhat elastic, but firm and strong. The players of this game do not throw the ball as a white man might do, instead, they drop it and at the same time kick it with their foot, using the instep for that purpose. The tallest men have the best chances in this game. Some of them will leap as high as five feet from the ground to catch the ball. The person who secures the ball kicks it. This continues for hours and the natives never seem to tire of the exercise.'

*The Marngrook Footy Show* first aired in 2007 on NITV (National Indigenous Television Network). It was devised by Grant Hansen after he realised there was not one Indigenous broadcaster or journalist working in mainstream footy media. Seeking to provide a solution to the problem, Grant's show instantly developed a cult following. Running for 90 minutes every Thursday night, *The Marngrook Footy Show* then switched to ABC2, before returning to NITV. Hosted by Hansen, with my great mate Gilbert McAdam as a regular panellist, alongside the wonderful Shelley Ware, the dynamic Derek Kickett, gifted Yolngu woman Leila Gurruwiwi and an array of regular guests, the show concluded in 2019 after a 12-year run, to be replaced by a series titled *Yokayi Footy* on SBS, co-hosted by new talent Megan Waters, the exuberant Bianca Hunt and Andrew Krakouer, who played 137 AFL games and is the son of Jimmy Krakouer. These programs provide constant visibility for Aboriginal television broadcasting talent, offering our insights as an extra dimension to the wealth of media time given to Aussie Rules nationally.

I've been invited to appear on both shows and have enjoyed the opportunity to participate in projects created and produced by my fellow Indigenous brethren. Similarly, it's a breath of fresh air to see the likes of Brooke Boney on the Nine Network's *Today* show, former AFL player and Best New Talent Logie Award winner Tony Armstrong on *ABC News Breakfast*, Rae Johnston on a variety of forums and Karla Grant on NITV. Rachel Perkins is a filmmaker who has created the doco series *First Australians*, the telemovie *Mabo* and the TV drama *Redfern Now*. I'm a fan of Leah Purcell, Aaron Pedersen, the mesmerising Miranda Tapsell and the outstanding acting skills of Deborah Mailman in every production she's been involved with, particularly the enthralling drama series with Rachel Griffiths titled *Total Control*.

Brick by brick, my people are building a wall of visibility across the media that was unimaginable when I was a kid.

Back then, in the 1960s and 1970s, we had the staggering presence of David Gulpilil in numerous films but, the occasional exception aside (including Tom E Lewis in *The Chant of Jimmie Blacksmith*), Gulpilil was pretty much a one-man representative.

Luckily that is being corrected and in AFL media we're seeing the likes of Shaun Burgoyne, Eddie Betts and Chris Johnson all making their mark in recent years.

Musically, Jessica Mauboy is a rightfully established and adored solo star, *Australian Idol* winner Casey Donovan has carved out her own space at the top of the musical theatre scene, Baker Boy didn't win five ARIA awards in 2022 by accident, and please, do me a favour (and if you haven't already), check out 'Milkumana', a song by the fast-rising surf rockers King Stingray from Arnhem Land whose self-titled debut album won the 2022 Australian Music Prize. You're most probably well-versed in the multifaceted creative named (Senator/Adam) Briggs, whose band is cleverly named A.B. Original (in which his musical partner is named Trials), but if not, please consider googling the updated version of 'Dumb Things' they did with Paul Kelly for Triple J's Like A Version, by way of introduction. Briggs has also written comedy for TV with Matt Groening of *The Simpsons*!

Bunjil, one of our spiritual creators, is spreading her international wings, people!

And, exactly 50 years after Evonne Goolagong Cawley won Wimbledon for her first of what became two London titles, I was so proud to see Ash Barty win Wimbledon herself, becoming the first Australian woman since Evonne to win it, and the second Indigenous person ever, of any gender. As unlikely, mathematically and psychologically, as it is for someone from the Indigenous community—which forms just the 3.8 per cent of this nation's population—to come from a vastly different culture into the AFL system and succeed, I can only imagine how much longer the odds of any of us mob succeeding internationally must be, no matter what the vocation. Whether it's Evonne, Ash, David Gulpilil, Cathy Freeman or the sublime singer–songwriter Gurrumul, I find myself becoming overawed when I consider how hard they've had to work to get the recognition they deserve.

I've been asked if I'm jealous of other Aboriginals earning their fair share of the spotlight and, to the contrary, my belief is that all ships rise with the tide.

# THIRTY-SEVEN

In February 2021, I was enjoying a quiet weekend lounging by a river in Nagambie, country Victoria, at a property owned by my loyal friend Gerry Ryan. It was a Monday night and a week or so earlier the *Herald Sun* had leaked a copy of the Collingwood footy club's own independently commissioned review on systemic racism within their organisation. Titled the 'Do Better Report', it followed consistent, detailed claims of bigotry from former premiership player Héritier Lumumba.

Collingwood had sat on the report for seven weeks since its findings were delivered on 11 December 2020. Then on 1 February 2021 the *Herald Sun* leaked the report. What it contained was a damning assessment on several fronts, the majority of which appeared to vindicate Héritier's often doubted allegations. Collingwood hastily called a press conference, during which, a suggestion was made that it was a proud day for the club.

That led to increasing calls for the club's president to step down, including in an open letter signed by over 70 well-known Indigenous Australians. Before the open letter was released, my peaceful riverside break was being constantly interrupted by dozens of phone calls, texts and emails from my Aboriginal brothers and sisters, asking me to add my name to the demand.

I get it. Ever since I lifted my jumper and pointed to my skin, I've been a media go-to guy for comments on racist footy incidents, and I'm usually happy to help, but it also puts me in the crosshairs of powerful people all over again, each and every time another race-based AFL story surfaces. I'm quietly living my daily life, before—BOOM! I'm besieged with requests for a comment. And it's not just powerful people I'm dragged in front of all over again. Nowadays, through social media, it's *all* people. Many of these people refuse to accept that the very concept of racism even exists, or they consider that those of us who are the targets should simply 'build a bridge and get over it'.

I wish it was that easy, believe me. I already made my point 30 years ago, and it still resonates because it mattered then and it matters now. My stance remains the same. Always was, always will be.

The other reason I usually prefer to lie low is that I don't consider myself to be clever. A racist incident almost always, by its very nature, involves some seriously heavy shit, which usually requires the ability to come up with a highly intellec-tual, educated response, which takes into account a variety of perspectives before arriving at a considered conclusion.

Whereas my first thought when hearing that somebody has, for example, thrown a banana over the fence at Eddie Betts is to wonder if we can find out where the person who did it lives. I can never be certain my comments won't make the situation worse and so I often choose to play it safe and say nothing at all.

I'm kind of ashamed to confess that I chose to stay out of the 'Do Better' debacle because I feared the repercussions of publicly speaking out against such influential individuals. The decades since I made my own spontaneous solo stand against racism have taken their toll. Héritier's stance was inspirational to me but I'd seen him suffer for his honesty, seen his claims be undermined and discredited, his legitimacy questioned, both by public figures and anonymous online trolls. I admired his courage, as others had told me they'd admired mine.

I'd earlier looked upon Adam Goodes as an equally brave and admired cultural leader, and still do. Adam's unwavering pride and Aboriginal advocacy often reduce me to tears.

But at that moment in Nagambie, as I reclined by that river, I didn't need to subject myself to the white-hot spotlight all over again.

On 22 April 2022, 15 months after the leaked 'Do Better Report', and following a variety of meetings with club officials regarding the application of recommendations made in the report, former players Héritier Lumumba, Andrew Krakouer and Leon Davis declared, in a statement on Twitter—'Nothing has changed. It is our firm belief that the Collingwood Football Club has no intention of acting in good faith to achieve a just outcome for past players who have experienced racism at the Club. [As a result] Leon Davis, Andrew Krakouer and I have formally notified the club that we are officially terminating all communications with CFC.'

Three months later, in July 2022, Davis and Krakouer made peace with Collingwood and became involved in building a culturally safe environment. Davis is employed by the club full-time, with Krakouer joining on a part-time basis.

Davis said in a club statement, 'I want to use my experiences of racism to better educate the community and better equip everyone with the knowledge, tools and education around our country's true history and why we still face the issues we do in today's society. We have the oldest living culture in the world and I encourage everyone to take it upon themselves to delve into that and to learn more about it. I'm pleased to be back.'

Credit where it's due too, because on 21 March 2023, Collingwood's Bobby Hill, an Indigenous small forward recruited from Greater Western Sydney over the summer, spoke highly of the club. 'I've never been in an environment like this before. It makes you feel like home walking in. It's an unbelievable feeling. Full credit to the staff, the players, the coaches. It makes life a lot easier.'

While I'll always stand with Héritier, ideally Bobby Hill's experience suggests there might be hope for the future.

In 1987, when I played my first game for St Kilda, 1.5 per cent of Australia's population was made up of Indigenous Australians. There was a total of 13 Indigenous AFL players on club lists that year, which was 2.5 per cent of all players.

Before my debut, only 39 Indigenous players had represented VFL/AFL teams.

In 1999, when I retired, there was a total of 45 Indigenous AFL players on club lists, which was 6.3 per cent of all players.

In 2023, there are 77 Indigenous AFL players on club lists, which is 9.8 per cent of all players.

Australia's entire Aboriginal and Torres Strait Islander population in 2023 forms just 3.8 per cent of the nation's population, so we are over-representing by a large margin in AFL circles.

In 2022 a host of Indigenous players, including Fremantle duo Michael Walters and Michael Frederick, Tigers pair Marlion Pickett and Maurice Rioli Jr, Melbourne's Kysaiah Pickett, Carlton's Adam Saad, Hawthorn's Chad Wingard and Brisbane's Callum Ah Chee, all reported instances of racial abuse. Perhaps I'm being grateful for small mercies but a possible positive way to view this information is that all those players felt able to speak publicly about it. In years past we were expected to suffer racism in silence but since the likes of myself, Michael Long, Adam Goodes, Héritier Lumumba and many others started speaking out, it seems we've created a pathway for all Indigenous footballers, black people, maybe all Indigenous Australian citizens, to feel comfortable doing the same.

# THIRTY-EIGHT

In recent years I've taken up painting as I find it relaxes me immensely. It eases my bouts of depression and anxiety and provides the solace I failed to achieve on the numerous occasions I've attempted meditation. My style is inspired by American artist Jackson Pollock, whose work has been described as abstract expressionist. I prefer to work outdoors, which is handy because I make an almighty mess during the process of creating my paintings. I believe the way I played football was a form of creativity and maybe that's why this artistic endeavour has been so cathartic for me.

I originally began dabbling for fun and it immediately felt so therapeutic, especially when I create by the river, with the wind rustling the leaves in the trees around me. As I got better I noticed people were making offers to buy my pieces as soon as they set eyes on them. The Mitchelton Gallery of Aboriginal

Art in Victoria displays some of my stuff and I exhibited 20 paintings in 2023 at Harrow in Victoria, home of the first Aboriginal cricket team (who went on to tour England in 1868), and birthplace of their best player, Johnny Mullagh, who was inducted into the Australian Cricket Hall of Fame in 2020.

My friend Lis Johnson, who helped Louis Laumen create my statue, is one of the best sculptors in the world, with her work on display outside the MCG and Rod Laver Arena among other prominent thoroughfares. Lis facilitated my interest in art by giving me paint and a canvas when I was annoying her one day in the studio. She has been consistently encouraging and is the main influence behind my improvement. She also acts as my artistic manager, refusing to take a cent in commission. Her sculpting skills are in demand internationally and she's recently declared that in future she will only create sculptures of Aboriginals and women.

I am pleased with my progress and continue to work hard. I was recently very proud to be selected as a finalist for the 2023 Gallipoli Art Prize.

My painting *Anzac Cove, Bombardment* began as an abstract exploration of colour and texture effects. During the painting I was fully immersed in the process, just following my intuitions.

Then as it reached completion, I started to see a powerful night-time sea and landscape, evocative of a wartime bombardment, both beautiful and terrifying.

*The Age* wrote:

For the past four years, Winmar has immersed himself in art. From virtually a standing start, under the tutelage of sculptor Lis Johnson, he has improved so rapidly that he is now a finalist in this year's prestigious Gallipoli Art Prize. Gallipoli Memorial Club President and Gadigal man John Robertson says, 'Winmar's inclusion on the 30th anniversary of his famous stand against racism is a poignant reminder of the contributions First Nations people have made to Australia's military history.'

You can view my creations @nickywinmarart on Instagram.

•

In 2021 I was honoured to be asked by the St Kilda Football Club to design their Indigenous Round jumper. I began by incorporating ancient rock art hand stencils I'd seen throughout WA on the back of the guernsey to represent connection to ancestors and unity between the Saints players who were to wear it. The front of the guernsey was a combination of three canvases I'd previously painted, including two willy-wagtails, my family totem, to represent both of my parents (or more broadly, parental hierarchy in general), alongside a silhouette of my moment at Victoria Park in 1993. Across these elements I applied the traditional Indigenous splatter technique.

While white people have star signs, aligned with astrology and attached to the date of their birth, Aboriginals have totems. A totem, in this context, is a natural object, plant or animal that is inherited by members of a clan or family as their spiritual emblem. In our culture, totems define people's roles and responsibilities, their relationships with creation and their affection for each other. Depending on where a person is from, they could have three or more totems that represent their nation and family group, as well as a personal totem if they wish. My family and I rely on just one, which is the willy-wagtail.

We call the wagtails *djitidjitis* (jiddyjiddys), after the sound they make. They are cheeky little birds, which you often see prancing around on the footy fields of the Western Australian area I am from. I believe every time I see two willy-wagtails together it is like Mum and Dad are coming back to talk to me and let me know they are safe and are thinking of me. These birds make me feel more relaxed and less alone in the world.

•

I've been playing the didgeridoo for many years now as it makes me feel directly connected to my ancestors. Cave paintings featuring people playing the didgeridoo suggest it may be mankind's oldest instrument, and it seems to have been around for at least as long as the 60,000 years Australian Indigenous people are known to have existed. When I play it, and I feel those deep vibrations surging through my body, I know I'm following in the tradition of my fellow tribal people going back centuries. Having a didgeridoo in my hands makes me feel secure and at home.

In 2022 I was invited to play the didgeridoo at the opening ceremony of the St Kilda versus North Melbourne game for the Sir Doug Nicholls Round. My cousin Fabian Winmar and I played a duet in front of a big crowd at Marvel Stadium. It was a magnificent moment for me. Any chance to maintain the profile of my people, to remind all Australians of our Indigenous history, is a worthy opportunity I'll always accept. As Sir Doug himself once said, 'You can get a piano tune from the black notes, a tune from the white notes, but to get harmony you have to play both.'

Before that, my most enjoyable personal musical experience was the night in July 2021 at Memo Music Hall (off Acland Street in St Kilda) when I happened to be strolling past in search of a good pizza joint and asked the bouncer who the band was that I could hear blasting out from inside. He told me it was Painters and Dockers, the 1980s punk band, doing a reunion gig. I'm friends with Paul Stewart, the lead singer, songwriter and long-time Melbourne journalist, who is a fantastic fella and once organised for me to meet the Godfather of Soul himself, the late great James Brown (James and I even had a kick of the Sherrin before his concert at Rod Laver Arena!). The bouncer at Memo Music Hall ushered me inside, then led me backstage, and within moments I was on the actual stage, singing their classic song 'Die Yuppie Die' to a full house. I'm not sure how I find myself in such unexpected scenarios so often but as that famous philosopher, Ferris Bueller, said, 'Life moves pretty fast. If you don't stop and look around once in a while, you could miss it.'

•

On 5 August 2022, Judith Durham, the lead singer of much-loved band The Seekers—who were the first Aussie musicians to crack the US and UK markets with record sales of over 50 million—sadly passed away. Her glorious vocal delivery of various smash-hit Seekers' songs will remain with us forever but it's 'The Future Australian National Anthem', a more inclusive version of 'Advance Australia Fair' that she co-wrote with Mutti Mutti man singer–songwriter Kutcha Edwards (the 2001 NAIDOC Awards Indigenous Person of the Year), which I will never forget.

Check out the suggested new interpretation and tell me it's not more representative of the Australia we know and love today.

In September 2022, a few weeks after Judith Durham sadly passed, I was on a road trip when I heard the familiar distinctive didgeridoo riff that kickstarts Goanna's superb 'Solid Rock', and up went the volume as far as it could go. Afterwards the radio DJ said the song was released '40 years ago today', and I had to pull the car over. How could four decades have passed since I'd heard that song performed on *Countdown* on our little black-and-white TV? Icons of my youth were ageing, dying or at death's door.

Australian cricket legend wicketkeeper Rod Marsh had passed away in March that year too. 'Caught Marsh, bowled Lillee' was a combination that devastated Australia's opponents for the best part of my upbringing, and Marsh was West Australian too. (I used to pretend to myself that 'Winmar to Lockett' might be the AFL equivalent of 'Caught Marsh, bowled Lillee').

Then Archie Roach departed, perhaps the most captivating Indigenous singer–songwriter of all time: a man who represented the Stolen Generations through his music and whose album *Charcoal Lane* is a masterpiece (his late wife Ruby Hunter was also a musical maestro in her own right). Archie also delivered me the ultimate honour by writing and releasing a song about my 'black and proud' moment, titled 'The Colour of Your Jumper'.

Archie's death was followed by that of Aboriginal elder, author, artist and activist Uncle Jack Charles.

My heroes and my peers are beginning to hit the deck in increasingly large numbers. I can feel my own mortality knocking at the door. Perhaps not at the door but I'm sure I heard the front gate creak open. Either way I'm in no mood to answer that door just yet. There's too much still to do.

I hope to enjoy seeing my people experience further cultural reparations, when and where they're warranted, and I hope to make more of my own personal reparations too.

I want to see my grandchildren grow up to become the sensible, kind and loving adults my own children became years ago.

Maybe one or more of those grandkids might one day follow in Grandad's footsteps and play for St Kilda (in the men's *or* women's teams). Perhaps they'll play in the Saints' premiership I long to witness before it's my turn to wave goodbye.

# THIRTY-NINE

The most recent example of an Indigenous sportsperson taking public pride in their pedigree was Jamarra Ugle-Hagan, the AFL's number one draft pick from 2020, as selected by the Western Bulldogs. In 2023, Jamarra had taken a few days away from the team after being subjected to racial abuse from an individual in the crowd the previous week. I was mortified to learn the racist fan had been a Saints supporter, but to St Kilda's credit they released a strong statement the very next day condemning vilification of any kind and saying, 'To be repeatedly addressing these repugnant instances of racism is a blight on our game and society. We will continue to stamp out and call out this unacceptable behaviour by having these important conversations, as well as make ongoing education available for the wider community.'

Jamarra returned days later, in time to play in Round 3. After kicking the game's first goal, he lifted his jumper and defiantly pointed to the colour of his skin. Again, I was bombarded by nearly 100 media people for a comment. Seeing as this instance was so obviously personally connected to me, and my famous moment, I made an exception via a one-off press release, which read:

I'm proud of Jamarra for standing up for himself. It's up to the new generations to reinforce the stance I made back in 1993. I'm still here, still involved with the issue, but it's been 30 years now, it's like a big relay race, time to pass on the baton.

I spoke to [the coach] Luke Beveridge today, to thank him for supporting Jamarra, and other Indigenous players at the Western Bulldogs. It's a great club, that I respect. I was welcomed and felt supported when I played for them in 1999.

Things are getting better, with increased awareness, and kids are getting educated in schools now about racism in sport and in society, which is great. There's still a few who can't control their negative attitudes, all we can do is keep supporting each other, and keep calling it out.

I also want to congratulate Jamarra for his outstanding on-field performance—5 goals, keep up the good work!

Nicky Winmar
Still black and proud
31st March 2023

•

The next night, on 1 April, St Kilda played their first home game at the MCG for as long as I can remember. The AFL agreed to the shift because 2023 is the 150th year of the St Kilda Football Club's existence. And in fact the very next day was the exact 150th year since the club was founded. Every living player who had ever pulled on the red, white and black Saints jumper was invited to the party. Hundreds of us were in attendance, and out on the hallowed MCG turf before the game, as the theme song was sung, former stars from days gone by were introduced to the nearly 70,000-strong crowd, a club record for a home-and-away round. A lot of the former players spoke of how it felt like we were attending our own wake, because so many of our families and friendship groups were together at the same place at the same time.

Nobody could have predicted (and in fact none of the professional pundits had) prior to the season that this Round 3, St Kilda versus Essendon, Saturday night game would be played by two of the top three teams on the ladder at that stage. Somehow the Saints, missing nine of their best 22, had won their first two games of the year.

During the off-season the club's administration had made an incredibly controversial move to sack coach Brett Ratten who they'd only re-signed three months earlier. In an unprecedented move on many counts, former coach Ross Lyon, under whom the Saints had previously played in three grand finals (without a premiership, alas), was brought back to hopefully finish the job he'd started more than a decade earlier. Every expert had projected the Saints to plummet further down the

2023 ladder than any other team, especially due to the spate of injuries they'd suffered to key players.

As I stood on the edge of the MCG's centre square, I felt tears welling as I recalled games won and lost, tackles that stuck, marks I'd taken and goals I'd kicked. All before big crowds in this cathedral, this colosseum of Australian sport. More than anything else, more than the dreams we dared to follow, more than the hopes that were dashed, I remembered the friendships forged out on the oval, the heartbeat of this city for more than a century. It was then I felt an arm wrap around me. I looked up and saw it was Tony Lockett who had embraced me. For a glorious, magnificent moment, I felt like I was home. Standing beside Plugger, in the middle of the grandest of all AFL stages, I sensed the love of my mum and dad, Kelly and our children, my grandchildren, every team-mate and every fan, everyone who's ever loved me, tried to love me, tolerated or been infuriated by me.

It helped that the Saints went on to rubber stamp the celebration with another win, making it a three from three new beginning.

•

On 18 April 2023, 30 years and one day since I took my stand, a traditional healing ceremony (or *Ngarra Jarra Noun*, Wurundjeri Woiwurrung for 'healing ceremony') was held at Victoria Park, on the same spot my moment occurred. The Kulin Nation people had historically considered the Victoria

Park land (before it was so-named) to be sacred territory, back when they were the area's only inhabitants.

The event was instigated and put together by former Essendon player Nathan Lovett-Murray and Jason Tamiru. It provided an opportunity for people who have suffered racism to heal through a ceremonial process that has been around for tens of thousands of years. It also provided an opportunity for deeper reflection and engagement by Indigenous and non-Indigenous Australians, ideally creating harmony and self-esteem by building relationships between black and white.

I've tried all sorts of therapy and haven't yet found the right type for me, but that healing ceremony went a long way towards putting a few ghosts to bed. Its purpose was to burn off and smoke out the bad blood that occurred on this patch of land, effectively cleansing it, and those who suffered trauma upon it. Traditional Aboriginal song and dance played a large part in the event, hundreds of friends and family flew in (among them, Leon Davis, Jeff Farmer, Des Headland and Robert Muir), and we welcomed the public to join us in looking forward towards a more unified society. Everyone who spoke (including Michael Long, Gilbert McAdam, Héritier Lumumba, new AFL boss Andrew Dillon, the current Collingwood captain Darcy Moore and current president Jeff Browne) helped my heart, and the hearts of others affected by the cruelty of racism, move closer towards healing.

Darcy Moore in particular asked to speak at the event and said, 'Thank you for having me. I really wanted to be here tonight. Nicky Winmar has an extraordinary legacy and he's had a powerful

285

impact on so many of us here. To see the young kids here today has really inspired me to keep working towards a shared future where we can all walk together in strength and solidarity.'

A week later Darcy sent me a Collingwood jumper, which was kind, but, y'know, even if I didn't have a historical problem with Collingwood, they *are* Collingwood after all. Before I threw it in the bin I noticed it had been signed by their entire current team, with a note expressing their love and respect for me. Damn it, I was touched by that gesture and so I've kept the bloody thing and I'll treasure it always.

Gilbert McAdam and I stayed close to each other through-out the evening, just as we've stayed close *with* each other since that diabolical day. Like our ancestors before us, we are survivors, and to stand on the same land where 30 years earlier we were vilified beyond belief, knowing the intention this time was to dispense with our demons, made us feel equal parts fragile and formidable.

Two days earlier, on 16 April, St Kilda played Collingwood as part of the AFL's hugely successful first ever 'festival of footy', titled Gather Round, during which every single game for that week was played over a long weekend in Adelaide. The AFL, in conjunction with the Magpies and the Saints, had arranged a commemoration of 'that day' back at Victoria Park, and I'd been flown in for the occasion. Collingwood surprised me that morning by offering a public apology, which read:

The Collingwood Football Club acknowledges it has been 30 years since Nicky Winmar lifted his jumper to say

'I'm black and I'm proud' after he and team-mate Gilbert McAdam were racially abused at Victoria Park.

Collingwood will play against St Kilda this afternoon and both clubs, together with the AFL, have worked together to ensure a respectful pre-game acknowledgement of the moment which took place on April 17, 1993.

Today, at Collingwood, we do not shy away from ensuring that racism is addressed when we see it or hear it.

The Collingwood Football Club understands that racism is harmful and has no place in our game and apologises to Nicky Winmar and to Gilbert McAdam for the hurt they experienced playing football.

It takes courage to stand against racism and when First Nations people do so, it is our opportunity—all Australians— to listen, learn and change for the better.

Collingwood also apologises for the appalling comments made by its most senior official in the days following that game.

To go back and reflect on where we got things wrong is important to us and we will continue to listen and learn as we progress our Club.

In 2020, the Club commissioned the Jumbunna Institute to conduct an independent review which resulted in the Do Better Report, challenging Collingwood to take action to confront racism. The Report concluded with 18 recommendations which the Club adopted and has since implemented.

In March last year, the Club shared the 12-month review of the work arising from the Do Better Report which noted that Collingwood had made 'significant and genuine progress'.

To be clear, we at Collingwood remain on a journey— we believe that real and lasting cultural change takes time, dedication and persistence.

We also believe there is no finishing line when it comes to eliminating racism.

Collingwood is incredibly fortunate to have many proud First Nations people who make up our Club across all levels—as players, coaches, staff and on our Board. We thank our First Nations brothers and sisters who continue to share their culture and experiences to make our Club better.

In recent weeks we have seen too many First Nations players racially vilified. There is still work to do.

Racism is never ok—it wasn't then, and it isn't now.

To Nicky Winmar, to Gilbert McAdam, and to their families, we say sorry.

Thank you, Collingwood.

Should I be angry that it has taken the Collingwood Football Club 30 years to officially offer an apology for the atrocity of their crowds? Nope, I reckon 'better late than never' is the healthy approach for me to take. And to the haters who spend their time setting up fake profiles on social media so they can send ugly untraceable abuse to black people? Well, I can't help but wonder, what do you possibly get out of it? My main man Elvis has three simple words for you: don't be cruel.

In the months leading up to the 30-year anniversary of my moment, various groups had been asking me to participate in a variety of commemorative events.

I started by politely declining and ended by being rude with my refusals, but I simply did not want to stir up all those old, awful emotions and memories yet again.

Eventually I decided a private reunion of the St Kilda players from that game back in 1993 would be the best bet, and so the Saints assisted me in setting up a casual sausage sizzle, washed down with a few quiet beers, at the club one afternoon in February. Eighteen of the 20 Saints who played that day were able to attend; we had the game playing on a big screen in the background and got all the guys to apply their handprints to a one-off artwork as a keepsake. I think we all got a lot of soul nourishment out of the day, and that's where I hoped it might all end.

Until Nathan Lovett-Murray, through his Indigenous Sports Network, suggested the healing ceremony and I couldn't help but jump at the concept. Between my private reunion in February and the healing event in April, the weight of media inquiries began to overwhelm me, as I feared they would. I sought out trusted friends to discuss whether I was doing myself—and the greater cause of trying to end (or at least reduce) racism—a disservice by refusing to participate in any major high-profile events surrounding the anniversary date. I'd previously impolitely rebuffed a couple of AFL forays, before I realised that, whether I liked it or not, my face and name would genuinely be able to have a positive impact on creating awareness of our need to continually push for a racism-free world.

I'm glad I agreed to go to Adelaide for the Gather Round because the pre-game activities focused upon preventing racism got a lot of attention nationally, and lifted my spirits as a result, rather than sending me spiralling emotionally and psychologically downhill, as I'd worried they might.

The St Kilda and Collingwood teams both ran through the same banner together before the game, which read 'Together We Stand. United Against Racism. Call It Out'. On the other side it read 'Nicky Winmar. 30 years on. Still black and proud'. Both teams formed a circle around me as I tossed the coin, and Collingwood's Indigenous players selected to play that day, Ash Johnson and Bobby Hill, presented me with ceremonial Indigenous gifts of friendship. The iconic Eddie Betts and I enjoyed a moving interview on the boundary for the television audience at home, which capped what really was one of the best days of my life. Who knew it would be topped only days later by the incredible healing ceremony experience? To have my son Tyson, my daughter Shakira, and her children—my grandchildren—attend that night made me choke up. I am eternally grateful to everyone who offered their support during those three events that surrounded the 30th anniversary.

After the kindness and reparations that Gilbert McAdam and I received during the Gather Round commemorative game, I began to tangibly feel degrees of accumulated stress lifting from my mind, an easing (not a removal) of the tightness in my chest, and (some of) the huge weight lifting off my shoulders. The official public apology from the Collingwood footy club, displaying that they have a conscience, and acknowledging wrongdoing, played a large part in that. The healing ceremony at Victoria Park contributed further to my increased sense of wellbeing. As did a group visit to Charcoal Lane (the street immortalised by Archie Roach as the title of his deadly debut album) the night before the ceremony, with family and friends who'd flown in especially for the healing event. People are generally well-meaning, and our fight to discourage the smaller yet persistent numbers of bigots continues, exhausting though it may be.

# FORTY

To be acknowledged by the AFL as an inductee to the game's Hall of Fame has really been the icing on the cake of my career. To be officially ranked alongside brother boys such as Adam Goodes, Peter Matera, Andrew McLeod and Stephen Michael, and my childhood North Melbourne heroes, such as Malcolm Blight, Keith Greig, David Dench and Ross Glendinning, is beyond a dream come true. To share this ultimate individual honour alongside my former team-mates Trevor Barker, Nathan Burke, Robert Harvey and Tony Lockett makes me feel amazing too.

Mum would have been able to enjoy the event because there was minimal chance of me getting injured by stepping on stage to accept the honour, and Dad would have been the proudest person on the planet.

In the taxi on the way home that night, I couldn't help but reflect on the fantastic voyage I'd been on, and it felt like I'd finally arrived at my destination.

Many of the wrong turns were all my fault, but I can't change the past. The positive stuff I can take some credit for, although I had a lot of assistance along the way.

When I think of the 1997 Grand Final, I just wish Dad could have hung in there for one more day. I'd have been better placed to ensure my beloved Saints won and I'd like to think a more focused me might have helped that happen.

I hold hope that incidents of racism will continue to be reduced, inside and outside of footy. I welcome the AFL's announcement this year that perpetrators of racist abuse at games will be banned for life (confirmed by Tanya Hosch after a massive petition was submitted by Nova Peris), and following the recent employment of Indigenous liaison people at all clubs, these decisions continue to further our hopes of a fear-free future. I look forward to seeing more First Nations people in administrative, coaching and mentoring roles within the AFL, which will ideally encourage, rather than discourage, young Indigenous talent to pursue and achieve their dreams, like I was lucky enough to do.

More broadly, I believe we are in safe hands with the Minister for Indigenous Australians, the Honourable Linda Burney, and the academic spokesperson Professor Marcia Langton, among many others wiser than I, representing our mob whenever it matters most. Their view is my view.

Nova Peris, one of my best friends, says, by embracing Indigenous Australians, white Australians won't lose 230 years of their history, they'll gain 60,000 years of history, and that's something we'd love them to be proud of, as we are.

As Nelson Mandela said, 'No one is born hating another person because of the colour of his skin, or his background, or his religion. People must learn to hate, and if they can learn to hate, they can be taught to love, for love comes more naturally to the human heart than its opposite.'

When I look at Wayne Ludbey's now famous 1993 photo, depicting the moment I chose to stand up for myself and my people, in the face of hostility, and I reflect upon the decades of attention that moment has drawn towards our fight to eliminate hate, I think, alongside my kids and grandkids, that's the proudest thing I ever helped happen in my life.

# ACKNOWLEDGEMENTS

To Matthew Hardy, who convinced me my story was worth telling, thank you for the love, patience, caution, concern and kindness you've shown as we put my life down on the page. Your own childhood memoir, *Saturday Afternoon Fever*, is a truly hilarious book.

To everyone at my brilliant publishers Allen & Unwin, in particular Jane Palfreyman, Tom Bailey-Smith, Jennifer Thurgate, Anabel Pandiella, Isabelle O'Brien, Deonie Fiford and Dannielle Viera.

Thank you especially to award-winning author and editor Wulli Wulli woman Lisa Fuller for her excellent cultural report on the manuscript. (We're thrilled that you loved it!)

I just know I'm going to forget people who I owe gratitude to regarding this book, so I apologise in advance, but here goes.

Among the many people I'd love to thank are Tynan, Shakira and their mum, Kelly, Benita and her mum, Frank Winmar, Cecil Winmar and Beth Hooper.

Thanks also to Gilbert McAdam, Tony Lockett, Gerry Ryan, Peter Jess, Doug Bear, Wayne Ludbey, Lazar Vidovic, Dean Greig, Graeme Gelllie, Stuart Trott, Nathan Lovett-Murray, South Fremantle Football Club, St Kilda Football Club, Western Bulldogs Football Club, every non-AFL club I've played for, Lis Johnson, Louis Laumen, Mick Hill, his wife, Liz, and kids Mitch and Chelsea, Luke Beveridge, the Ivanhoe Hotel, all my coaches (including Kevin White and Kevin Casterton at Pingelly), all my team-mates, all my fellow Indigenous footballers, Russell Holmesby, Bruce Eva, Tanya Hosch, Brian Walsh, Meshel Laurie, Peter Dixon, Gil McLachlan, Andrew Dillon, Matt Finnis, Simon Lethlean, Aunty Katrina Amon, Jenny Lalor and Julia Zemiro.

To Mick Molloy, Sam Pang and Andy Maher from *The Front Bar* and to Mark Robinson and Gerard Whateley from *AFL 360* on Fox Footy (plus all their producers and staff).

And thank you to the Humphries, Winmar and Abrahams families, Cliff and Muriel Collard and family, Georgie Day, Alan Davis, Richard Walley, Ian Silk, Paul Konstanty, Karen Bunting, Tony Morris, Simon and Mark Hardy, Jason Hynes, Adrian Skepper, Greg Swedosh, Linda Burney, Nova Peris, Danny Frawley (My Captain) and Anita Frawley.

# RECORDS

VFL Team of the Year/All-Australian 1989, 1991, 1995

AFL Hall of Fame, inducted 2022

309 senior games, 415 goals

58 games, 98 goals for South Fremantle, 1983–86

230 games, 283 goals for St Kilda, 1987–98

21 games, 34 goals for Western Bulldogs, 1999

8 State of Origin games for Western Australia, 10 goals

St Kilda Best and Fairest 1989, 1995

St Kilda leading goal-kicker, 1988

St Kilda Team of the Century

Indigenous Team of the Century

Western Australia Team of the Century

South Fremantle Team of the Century

# RESOURCES

**Should you wish to assist Michael Long's and
Danny Frawley's marvellous charities, check out:**
thelongwalk.com.au
michaellongfoundation.org.au
saints.com.au/spud

**To seek help:**
beyondblue.com.au
1300 22 4636

***The Ripple Effect***
afl.com.au/ondemand/original/651280/the-ripple-effect

# INDEX

# INDEX